T0316608

Employee Engagement

The field of employee engagement has experienced unprecedented growth over the last three decades. Despite remarkable progress in both practice and scholarship, there remains tremendous confusion about what employee engagement is, what it means, and how organizations can take proactive steps to harness the full power of an engaged workforce.

This short-form book provides readers a unique and research-based road map through the rapidly evolving research around employee engagement, including the identification of key literature and theory along with expert, timesaving connections to how theory has informed practice. The author covers the various disciplinary approaches and schools of thought, thematically bridging scholarly literature – including and identifying the historically significant and most current – to better understand how the research is evolving and what new opportunities for scholarship are emerging.

Essential reading for scholars of human resource management, leadership and management more broadly, the book is also a valuable read for reflective practitioners globally.

Brad Shuck is Associate Professor of Organizational Leadership and Learning at the University of Louisville, USA.

State of the Art in Business Research
Edited by Professor Geoffrey Wood

Recent advances in theory, methods, and applied knowledge (alongside structural changes in the global economic ecosystem) have presented researchers with challenges in seeking to stay abreast of their fields and navigate new scholarly terrains.

State of the Art in Business Research presents short-form books which provide an expert map to guide readers through new and rapidly evolving areas of research. Each title will provide an overview of the area, a guide to the key literature and theories, and time-saving summaries of how theory interacts with practice.

As a collection, these books provide a library of theoretical and conceptual insights, and exposure to novel research tools and applied knowledge that aid and facilitate in defining the state of the art, as a foundation stone for a new generation of research.

Strategic Human Resource Management
A Research Overview
John Storey, Dave Ulrich and Patrick M. Wright

Flexible Working in Organizations
A Research Overview
Clare Kelliher and Lilian M. de Menezes

Network Industries
A Research Overview
Matthias Finger

Strategic Risk Management
A Research Overview
Torben Juul Andersen and Johanna Sax

For more information about this series, please visit: www.routledge.com/State-of-the-Art-in-Business-Research/book-series/START

Employee Engagement
A Research Overview

Brad Shuck

Routledge
Taylor & Francis Group

LONDON AND NEW YORK

First published 2020 by Routledge

2 Park Square, Milton Park, Abingdon, Oxon OX14 4RN
605 Third Avenue, New York, NY 10017

Routledge is an imprint of the Taylor & Francis Group, an informa business

First issud in paperback 2021

British Library Cataloguing-in-Publication Data
A catalogue record for this book is available from the British Library

Library of Congress Cataloging-in-Publication Data
A catalog record for this book has been requested

ISBN: 978-1-138-49060-4 (hbk)
ISBN: 978-1-03-217740-3 (pbk)
DOI: 10.4324/9781351035064

Typeset in Times New Roman
by Apex CoVantage, LLC

Contents

Employee engagement: a research-based overview of the theory and practice

Key Words: Employee engagement; job engagement; work engagement; engagement; performance; human resource management; human resource development; human resource; organization development; organizational development; performance; affect

1 The case for employee engagement

In 1990, William Kahn published his now seminal work on *personal engagement* and *disengagement*, igniting decades of research and practice – all to harness and better understand this idea of employee engagement. Post 1990, research on engagement has developed into a field of dedicated and growing study in multiple areas of practice. Employee engagement has clearly captivated the attention of scholars and practitioners across the globe. A sure sign of this growth and attention has been the burgeoning of research over just the last decade, including a global boom of research focused toward understanding the application, theory development, and measurement of employee engagement. After making its official debut in 1990, the field of engagement has matured to include multiple perspectives, frameworks of measurement, and at times, competing theoretical models.

Despite remarkable progress across varying streams of intersecting literature bases, there remains tremendous confusion about what employee engagement is, what it means in both research and practice, and how organizations can take proactive steps to harness the full power of a fully engaged workforce. From an academic standpoint, voluminous research dots the landscape, yet most streams of literature remain disjointed and fragmented. From a practice standpoint, few leaders understand employee engagement in a way that is actionable. Notwithstanding this problem, there is, however, a growing clarity about engagement-linked states and distinctions between ideas, particularly the positionality of employee engagement (Shuck *et al.*, 2016b; Saks and Gruman, 2014). This book provides a brief overview of that development and chronicles the construct historically, offering a structure for cataloguing the field's growth as well as providing an overview of the multiple facets that make up the present state of employee engagement theory and research today. Along the way, this book is built on an anthology of important works by identifying the seminal and most emergent work in the field, as a way to streamline and make meaning of the literature for interested readers and practitioners who want to know more about employee engagement.

Perhaps surprising, despite decades of research, employee engagement remains a contentious and at times controversial topic. Researchers have questioned if employee engagement is redundant with job satisfaction and other like job attitudes (Newman and Harrison, 2008; Newman *et al.*, 2011), if engagement can be measured accurately (Keenoy, 2013), and whether or not engagement is just another stream of corporate propaganda designed to exploit employees to get them to work harder for the sake of profitability (Guest, 2014). These are all questions that should be critically examined, and this unique book is an endeavor to overview the breadth of employee engagement research and the new ideas emerging across the globe, including tackling these challenging questions head-on.

Despite critical inquiry, as a phenomenon, there is no denying that employee engagement has been a significantly trending topic in both the management and human resource fields for decades. According to the most recent Google Scholar trends, the topic of employee engagement is as popular as it has ever been. See Figure 1.1.

Figure 1.1 represents a Google Trend line tracking the total level of search interest relative to the highest point on the chart for a given length of time – in this case, 2004 to early 2019. A value of 100 represents the peak of popularity for the term across time. The Google Trend score for employee engagement is 99. Interest in employee engagement has never been higher. For comparison, when juxtaposed alongside the search terms *work engagement* and *job engagement*, two very popular and often synonymously used terminologies, the fervor of interest in employee engagement is quite clear. See Figure 1.2 for a comparison. It's not even close. The idea of employee engagement is enormously popular, and all signs point toward increasing significance worldwide.

It seems everyone wants more employee engagement, yet little research is able to precisely articulate how the experience develops in practice. Awareness remains high, but our understanding remains decidedly low. More, in recent years, a myth that global engagement is on the decline has circulated (Scott, 2017). Even Gallup's own *State of the American Work-force* has highlighted stagnant levels of engagement since early 2010. This is a seemingly significant problem. How is it that scholars have researched employee engagement for decades, dissected nearly every angle of the construct, looked at outcomes as well as catalogued antecedents and drivers, and still engagement levels remain stagnant almost 20 years running? Perhaps we are missing something in the engagement dilemma. This issue must be addressed.

This dilemma raises questions about the present state of the employee engagement field and its future trajectory. While employee engagement has developed into a multi-streamed conversation, there remain debates

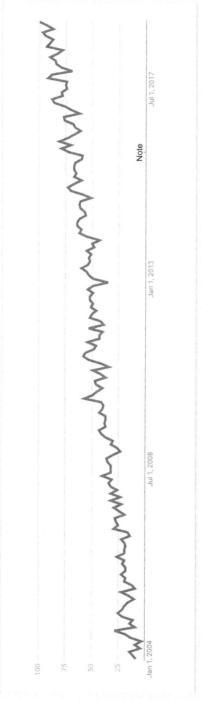

Figure 1.1 Level of interest in the search term *employee engagement*

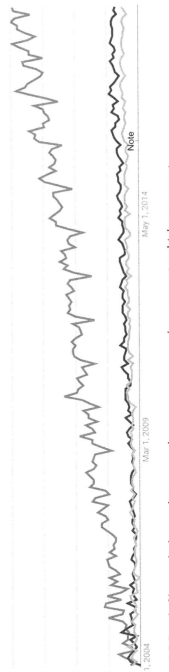

Figure 1.2 Level of interest in the search terms *employee engagement, work engagement,* and *job engagement*

and disagreement about how best to frame and represent what we mean as scholars when we say *employee engagement* (Saks and Gruman, 2014). For example, how is employee engagement best positioned, how can we make sense of the inter-connected conversations that scholars are having, what does the history of employee engagement tell us about its future, and how does this domain of scholarship best fit within the human resource and management literature moving forward? More, how do we make sense that despite voluminous records of research, we know very little about what employee engagement actually is all the while global consultancies (c.f., Hewitt, 2015) continue suggesting that employee engagement is either stagnant or on a steep decline?

As the field of employee engagement develops, scholars and practitioners should take stock in the historical landscape and then look to the future – and connect the two with intentionality. Traditionally speaking, and in contrast to other like constructs, the field of research that encapsulates employee engagement is relatively young and perhaps just starting to peak. Considering that research on similar variables such as job satisfaction and organizational commitment date back several decades, employee engagement is a new, still emerging idea. Yet, employee engagement – as an idea – seems to have the potential to impact some of our greatest challenges in the workplace, and the research has been clear on the influence of engagement toward critical business outcomes (Harter *et al.*, 2002; Harter *et al.*, 2010; Xanthopoulou *et al.*, 2009). If this is at all true – that employee engagement has the potential to impact practice in real ways – how then, will employee engagement influence the emerging landscape of organizations over the next millennia, and how will work and the working context be shaped over time through this lens?

To better explore these questions, the remainder of this book comprises five chapters. Chapter 2 offers a history of definitions and speaks directly to what the research says employee engagement is and what it is not, wading through the building wave of scholarship published over the past three decades. Chapter 3 highlights the expression of employee engagement and speaks to the makeup of engagement from a cognitive, emotional, and behavioral framework. Chapter 4 considers emerging trends and the future of the field, particularly as it relates to measurement. Chapter 5 discusses the documented impact of engagement from an organizational, individual, and health and wellness perspective, linking the state of employee engagement to important and critical societal factors including burnout. Finally, Chapter 6 puts closure on this conversation by highlighting emerging areas of development, the reality of disengagement, and offering brief closing remarks on the individual state of employee engagement.

I should point out that you do not need to read this book in progressive order. Each chapter can be read individually and out of order without losing too much significance. Cover to cover. Ala carte. Buffet-style. However you prefer. My hope is that you read this book in a way that is helpful and significant to you. If you are a practitioner and want more information about how to measure engagement, Chapter 4 would be a great starting point. If you are a scholar looking for grounded theoretical frameworks on employee engagement for a paper you are writing, you might consider starting at Chapter 3 and then going back for more detail in Chapters 2 and 5. If you are a student of employee engagement, I hope you might read every word cover to cover. However you use this book, I hope that it is helpful and thought-provoking.

As a final note, this book is limited by what I know, what could be found, as well as my own personal perspective and connection to the theory. To be sure, this book takes a decidedly psychological perspective to understanding employee engagement. There are, of course, other frames of reference – economic, political, historical, etc. – but this book accounts for the human being in the natural working environment. I do not pretend to have read everything about employee engagement and included it here, to know all of the nuances, or even to be able to divorce myself from my own sense of reality when it comes my own experiences of engagement. Rather, I believe these chapters provide the groundwork for understanding the structure, discourse, and future of the employee engagement field, all grounded in the existing literature. Interested readers should consult root citations, read the original articles for more detail, and critically explore the story being told.

I hope you are inspired. And more, I hope you remain engaged.

2 What exactly is employee engagement?

There are many documented, well-cited sources of existing research on employee engagement. They include seminal (Kahn, 1990; Saks, 2006; Maslach *et al.*, 2001; Schaufeli *et al.*, 2002; Schaufeli *et al.*, 2006; Shuck, Rocco, & Albornoz, 2011b; Shuck and Wollard, 2010) and current scholarly articles (Shuck *et al.*, 2016a; Shuck *et al.*, 2016b; Potgieter, 2016; Shuck *et al.*, 2017a; Bailey *et al.*, 2017; Saks and Gruman, 2014; Purcell, 2014; Valentin, 2014; Kahn and Heaphy, 2014; Briner, 2014; O'Boyle *et al.*, 2012; Cole *et al.*, 2012) as well as edited volumes (Albrecht, 2010; Truss *et al.*, 2013a), practitioner white papers (Wildermuth, 2008; Hewitt, 2015), and books (Wagner, 2015; Kelleher, 2013). This chapter will focus on the meaning of employee engagement and the historical development of its definition through a review of connected literature – including many of those cited above – and will offer a glimpse into the etymology of employee engagement through a specific and research grounded definition.

Notwithstanding the many documented sources of existing literature, the interested reader would be hard pressed to find two different authors who used the same definition, positionality, or even meaning. As a result, the meaning of engagement has remained unapologetically disconnected throughout its existence. Scholars have routinely applied varying definitions, frameworks, and terms meant to bring clarity, but unfortunately, their use has resulted in misunderstanding. This has been, in review of the historical development of the engagement construct, out of a good faith effort to bring the construct forward, yet, misunderstanding remains. Throughout this chapter, the dominant perspectives of employee engagement are detailed and then juxtaposed alongside like constructs such as job engagement and work engagement, as well more emergent constructs such as collective engagement, social intellectual engagement, and organizational engagement. A variety of definitions are provided throughout this chapter to be clear about what is meant when terms are used in both research and practice. As a tool to provide a streamlined perspective of the varying definitions in one central place, Table 2.1 provides an overview of the terms used throughout the chapter including the engagement-type name, the root citation of the original work, and a specific definition, quoted directly from the originating, root-citation author.

Despite the attempt at meaning making throughout this chapter, debate about positionality and definitional clarity will likely remain ardent for years to come – well beyond this book. Nonetheless, in what follows is a historical depiction and analysis of the employee engagement construct to date, offering readers a look back in time and perhaps, a glimpse into the future.

The meaning of employee engagement

Across the spectrum of three decades, there have been many definitions of engagement proposed in the literature. See for example the exemplars in Table 2.1. Nested within this table, is the term employee engagement. Employee engagement has been defined as the *maintenance, intensity,* and *direction of cognitive, emotional, and behavioral energy* (Shuck *et al.*, 2017c). This definition offers several distinguishing factors that set it apart as unique from other like constructs such as job engagement (Rich *et al.*, 2010) and work engagement (Schaufeli, 2013; Schaufeli *et al.*, 2006; Schaufeli *et al.*, 2002). For example, this specific definition of employee engagement is connected to early work by Shuck and Wollard (2010) as well as emergent and more recent research by Shuck *et al.* (2016b) and Nimon *et al.* (2016a). These sources each specifically focus on *employee engagement* and build toward a connected, streamlined understanding of the construct.

More, this definition denotes that in its full state, engagement requires three unique features – first, the maintenance of energy, suggesting that employee engagement is (a) active, stable, and steady; (b) that the experience of employee engagement varies (or can vary) in intensity based on individual interpretation of a single experience or series of experiences; and last, (c) engagement has some level of directionality – that is, employee engagement does not happen in a vacuum, but rather is targeted at something, someone, or toward someplace through intention. Employee engagement is uniquely focused in a working context and captures the full involvement of an individual's work including the psychological experience of work and working, which makes up what it means to be engaged in actual practice (Shuck *et al.*, 2017c).

The Shuck *et al.* definition of employee engagement was derived by tracing the research roots back through the historical literature starting with the ideas and frameworks of *personal engagement* proposed

Table 2.1 Historical overview of engagement-type, definitions, and root citations

Engagement-Type Name	Definition of Engagement	Root Citation of Original Work
Personal Engagement	"Simultaneous employment and expression of a person's 'preferred self' in task behaviors that promote connections to work and to others, personal presence, and active full role performances" (p. 700)	Kahn, W. (1990). Psychological conditions of personal engagement and disengagement at work. *The Academy of Management Journal, 33*(4), 692–724. doi: 10.2307/256287
Employee Engagement	Employee engagement has been defined as the *maintenance, intensity*, and *direction of cognitive, emotional, and behavioral energy* (Shuck et al., 2017c)	Shuck, B., Osam, K., Zigarmi, D. and Nimon, K. 2017c. Definitional and conceptual muddling: Identifying the positionality of employee engagement and defining the construct. *Human Resource Development Review*, 16, 263–293. 10.1177/1534484309353560
Work Engagement	"A positive, fulfilling, work-related state of mind that is characterized by vigor, dedication, and absorption" (p. 74)	Schaufeli, W. B., Salanova, M., González-Romá, V., and Bakker, A. B. (2002). The measurement of engagement and burnout: A two sample confirmatory factor analytic approach. *Journal of Happiness Studies, 3*(1), 71–92. doi: 10.1023/A:1015630930326
Job Engagement	"Multi-dimensional motivational concept reflecting the simultaneous investment of an individual's physical, cognitive, and emotional energy in active, full work performance" (p. 619)	Rich, B. L., Lepine, J. A., and Crawford, E. R. (2010). Job engagement: Antecedents and effects on job performance. *Academy of Management Journal, 53*(3), 617–635. doi: 10.5465/amj.2010.51468988

originally by Kahn (1990). This notion of personal engagement is widely credited by engagement scholars to be the first academic example to name an engagement-type behavior in a working context and is the original root citation of the construct we know as employee engagement.

Engagement as active

Through his ground-breaking, original research, Kahn explored the meaning and application of engagement through the lenses of psychology and sociology beginning with the classic text, *The Presentation of Self in Everyday Life* (Goffman, 1961). In this work, Goffman argued that a human's attachment and detachment to life roles varied depending on a person's interactions during everyday fleeting, moment-to-moment, face-to-face (or context-to-context) encounters. Connected, Kahn proposed that when individuals were at work – or while being in work – "[they] act[ed] out momentary attachments and detachments in role performances" (Kahn, 1990, p. 694). This interactionalist idea greatly influenced the early formation and understanding of what engagement was and provided scholars a direct reference to Goffman's (1961) theory that was specific to the workplace as well as grounded in a mature field of study (i.e., sociology). More, the intentional interplay – as well as ebb and flow – between the individual and their work-based context underscored the psychological perspective of early engagement theory (Kahn, 1990), including later commentary (c.f., Kahn, 2010; Kahn and Heaphy, 2014).

Kahn's early work on personal engagement

To derive his work, Kahn (1990) interviewed 32 employees – 16 summer camp counselors and 16 financial professionals – using a qualitative ethnographic, grounded theory approach. The main focus of his work was to explore individual work experiences with various work variables (i.e., manager satisfaction, role clarity, availability of resources) to best understand how the experience of work and work-based conditions influenced the outcomes of work, and thus effort toward work, an action he later called *engagement*.

Kahn defined personal engagement as "the simultaneous employment and expression of a person's 'preferred self' in task behaviors that promote connections to work and to others, personal presence, and active full role performances" (p. 700). Influenced by Goffman, Kahn also relied on several now seminal texts in fields such as in psychology (Freud, 1922), sociology (Merton and Merton, 1968), group theory (Slater, 1966; Smith and Berg, 1987), social identity theory (Ashforth and Mael, 1989), job stress theory (Thoits, 1991), job design technology (Hackman and Oldham, 1980), as well as emerging literature on emotion in the workplace (Hochschild, 1979) to round out his theoretical frame. Kahn offered that engagement in work was a motivational variable spanning the extrinsic and intrinsic continuum, which promoted the use of an employee's full self in their work roles. He called this *personal engagement* and *personal disengagement*. His theory was hinged on three specific conditions of the work experience. In short, according to Kahn, for full engagement to be present, experiences of work had to be (a) meaningful, (b), reasonably safe, and (c) resourced proportionately (i.e., an employee would believe that they had the relative resources to do the work expected of them at a proportionate and reasonable level). The more an employee believed their work had meaning, that their work was safe, and that they had the resources required to complete their work, the more likely they were to be engaged in their work – and vice versa. The sum of these three experiences were believed to capture what it meant to be personally engaged in work physically, emotionally, and cognitively (Rich *et al.*, 2010). See Chapter 3 for more details on this connection.

Contemporary perspectives on personal engagement: grounding engagement as an active condition

In later commentary, Kahn (1992) reconsidered the meaning of psychological presence in work as a direct extension of the meaningfulness, safety, and availability conditions he had outlined previously. Being present was about believing in the meaning of work, believing that work was safe (physically, emotionally, and cognitively [Rich *et al.*, 2010]), and trusting that support was present to complete that work. Being fully present in work was positioned to be the meaning of living life to its fullest. "When fully present, people feel joined with someone outside themselves; they experience themselves as accessible to people or tasks, as reserves to be drawn on" (p. 326).

In more present commentary on the nature of Kahn's work, Christian *et al.* (2011) observed that across the gamut of engagement research, the issues of a pull toward "performance of work tasks" and "self-investment of personal resources" (p. 91) were central to what was meant when Kahn used the term *engagement*. Being present was, according to broad interpretation, a function of being engaged and the balance of an employee's core beliefs about how meaningful, safe, and resource available their work context was at the very moment of engagement or disengagement. This observation by Christian *et al.* (2011) was centered in Kahn's (1990) early work and highlighted a common core belief about what engagement was across two decades of emerging research. Employee engagement emerged in both theory and practice as an active, present, and involved self-discretion of resources toward something.

Across a survey of historical engagement definitions (see Table 2.1), scholars and practitioners seem in some accord that the phenomenon of employee engagement involves an *active* pull forward and toward performance and that being engaged is an active experience and not a passive condition (c.f., Parker and Griffin, 2011; Schaufeli *et al.*, 2011).

Employee engagement is forward moving not stationary (Biggs *et al.*, 2014). This positioning of engagement as active is one of the earliest distinguishing features of the employee engagement construct found throughout the research literature.

Engagement as stable: trait, state, or trait-state

When it comes to the stability of engagement, there has been significant debate about whether engagement is best positioned as a state or as a trait. Macey and Schneider (2008) were some of the first scholar-practitioners to wade into this conversation. In a significant departure from Kahn, Macey and Schneider suggested that employee engagement was best understood as three unique forms of engagement – all different from one another yet associated in relationship: (a) *trait engagement*, (b) *state engagement*, and (c) *behavioral engagement* (2008). From this perspective, employee engagement was defined by suggesting that "(a) job design attributes . . . directly affect[ed] trait engagement, (b) the presence of a transformational leader . . . directly effect[ed] state engagement, and (c) the presence of a transformational leader . . . directly affect[ed] trust levels and thus, indirectly affect[ed] behavioral engagement" (Macey and Schneider, 2008, p. 25).

In their model, a preceding state of engagement was believed to build on the next, with each independent state developing the next experience in the engagement-chain. Now regarded as a seminal conceptual work, Macey and Schneider may have inadvertently introduced murkiness into the employee engagement field by confusing traits, states, and behaviors, all on one framework and through one definition, which remains a contested matter across the spectrum of research on employee engagement to date.

The trait engagement perspective: engagement as stable or flexible

Several researchers have explored engagement as a trait (Langelaan *et al.*, 2006; Wildermuth and Mello, 2010), as some form of trait-related affect or emotion (Dalal *et al.*, 2012), or as a trait embedded within a psychological state. This differentiation has been mired in academic nuance and detail for decades and as a result, many engagement scholars have chosen not to wade into this conversation at all – they simply avoid it. The debate has, however, been contentious and confusing, yet the perspective and understanding of the Macey and Schneider proposition has implications for researchers and practitioners.

For example, if engagement is defined as a trait, or as trait-like (Macey and Schneider, 2008), there are consequences for this positioning in both time and context for how engagement is enacted in practice (Shuck et al., 2017c). If we say that engagement is a trait, this means that employees are born to be engaged or not engaged, rather than experience engagement as a developed social or psychological phenomenon through some contextual interpretation. In support of this view, recent meta-analytic work by Young *et al.* (2018) suggested that positive affectivity was a strong predictor of employee engagement (31.10% of the explained variance; $\rho = .62$), followed by proactive personality (19.60%; $\rho = .49$), conscientiousness (14.10%; $\rho = .39$), and extraversion (12.10%; $\rho = .40$). In parallel earlier work, Wildermuth and Mello (2010) suggested that underlying personality characteristics such as neuroticism, extraversion, and conscientiousness (FFM; Judge *et al.*, 2002) could predispose employees to experience high levels of engagement lending support to work by both Rich (2006) and Langelaan *et al.* (2006) who both supported the possible impact of personality traits on employee engagement.

Some scholars have been critical of this positioning, however. Shuck *et al.* (2017c), for example, argued that if we take trait theorists at their word – that is, only people with a proactive personality, who are conscientiousness and extraverted can be engaged – engagement is then an innate disposition of personality, and no amount of development or organizational change management effort could nudge employees to be more engaged. Leaders must then hire for engagement through predictive indexes and personality assessments. Indeed, in their work, Young *et al.* (2018) endorsed personality-based selection as a viable means for building teams with highly engaged employees and they discuss the implications for using personality assessment to select engaged employees. This remains a highly controversial, and perhaps illegal, practice.

At present, only a small handful of studies have rigorously explored the influence of personality characteristics on the emergence of employee engagement, and the amount of empirical evidence linking personality traits and engagement is, at least at this time, insufficient to make a definitive claim. However, while few scholars fully subscribe to this trait-based positioning only, the few who do provide an important perspective for understanding the full field of engagement research.

Considering the evidence provided throughout the literature, it seems possible – even likely – that perceptions of work environment conditions could be shaped by job perceptions and job perceptions shaped by personality dispositions. Trait engagement (Young *et al.*, 2018) likely exerts some influence on the ways in which employees interpret their work environment. Mood and attitude matter, and there remains a voluminous record of research that has explored the impact of personality on a host of outcomes related to performance. On the other hand, and connected directly back to early work on personal engagement, a second positioning around employee engagement as a state has dominated the prevailing literature on employee engagement in recent years.

The state engagement perspective: engagement as directionality

The state engagement perspective is very different from the trait-based perspective. Specifically, while the trait-based perspective suggests that engagement is a function of personality or disposition, the state-based perspective offers that instead of being stable, it is in constant flux, building or eroding over time in proportion to an experienced moment, or series of moments and individual interpretation of those moments (Xanthopoulou *et al.*, 2012).

As a compliment to the trait-based perspective, the concepts of stability and persistence are important ideas to consider when exploring engagement. For example, throughout the research literature, many scholars have routinely positioned engagement as an experience that is – at its core – a psychological state and adaptable in the moment (Xanthopoulou *et al.*, 2012; Ouweneel *et al.*, 2012; Garg *et al.*, 2018; Bailey *et al.*, 2017; Fletcher *et al.*, 2017; Shuck *et al.*, 2016a; Owens *et al.*, 2016; Saks and Gruman, 2014; Kahn and Heaphy, 2014; Truss *et al.*, 2013b). This theoretical positioning allows for flux and variation – versus disposition, which is fixed. This is what we experience as employee engagement in the moment we are engaged.

Under normal conditions, a leader would likely not expect engaged employees to suddenly appear in a meeting room, and while a hiring manager might be able to screen for dispositions that are more engagement-like, the research would suggest that the conditions of climate at work matter and also influence the full experience of engagement, driving where and how an employee becomes engaged. An employee who believes that the time they spend in a meeting is a meaningless activity is unlikely to be engaged no matter what their disposition is. They see the activity as empty and fruitless. The state of the context lacks meaning and thus, drives direction of the state. One of the more commonly misunderstood characteristics of engagement is that it is not boundless. There are limits to engagement and an employee cannot be engaged in two places at once, and while they may not be engaged in the meeting, they are engaged in something else – perhaps thinking about how to get out of the meaningless event, or what they will be doing afterwards.

Engagement scholars have routinely suggested that it is often not one meaningless meeting (or any activity that is work-centric) that spurs energy toward the direction of disengagement (see Chapter 6 for more details on disengagement), or non-engagement, but likely a long line of meetings (or whatever cumulative context may be present) interpreted as conditionally meaningless over time. The experienced phenomenon of engagement is not a singular interaction or interpretation in any one direction or another (Xanthopoulou *et al.*, 2012), but rather a series of experiences connected to a building context over time, defined as the maintenance of the energy that is engagement. If engagement is influenced by interpretation, then it must be at least minimally influenced by context, positioning the experience as a psychological state which has directionality. The maintenance of that state of engagement (the psychological experience) builds over time, and this flux is known in the research literature as the *cumulative effect* (i.e., Shuck, 2018).

Employee engagement: maintenance, direction, and intensity

The state engagement perspective demonstrates that the persistence of an individual's level of engagement over time stems from the meaning that work or job activities have for an individual (Xanthopoulou *et al.*, 2012). Over the course of the field, many scholars have reliably recommended that contextual meaning in work and of work has a natural flow (Bledow *et al.*, 2011; Kahn, 1990; Saks and Gruman, 2014; James *et al.*, 2011). This ebb and flow requires a maintenance of condition, which directs levels of intensity (how hard someone works) and the direction of the output (what work gets done), connecting with the definition offered by Shuck *et al.* (2017c). Employee engagement involves not heightened levels of work intensification (working hard for the sake of working hard), but rather a momentary motivational *state*, grounded in the interpretation of conditions, depicted by an intensity of energy toward a work target (i.e., directionality) within a context that an individual experiences as meaningful, safe, and resource adequate (Brown and Leigh, 1996; James *et al.*, 2011). This provides maintenance of the experience and direction of the outcome.

In sum, scholars on both sides have explored employee engagement from both a trait-based as well as state-based perspective. The definitions in Table 2.1 provide a historical view of how employee engagement has been defined, as well as how it has matured in the research literature.

Up through this point, Chapter 2 has detailed and cross-referenced the historical development of employee engagement, taking special care to connect definition to both seminal and emergent literature. While this chapter has been focused toward what employee engagement is, by way of definition, across the research literature scholars have routinely used terms meant to describe engagement interchangeably. At times, and much like Macey and Schneider, this has added confusion to the meaning of employee engagement and other engagement-like terms. In the next section, we look more closely into what employee engagement is not and briefly overview the differences in these terms.

What employee engagement is not

Within the literature, employee engagement has been called many things. Scholars have worked to disentangle the meaning of engagement and define both what it is and what it is not. For example, employee engagement has been both acclaimed as essential for performance (Christian *et al.*, 2011) and simultaneously criticized as being redundant (Newman *et al.*, 2011). In the following sections, similar constructs are reviewed alongside employee engagement to distinguish what the research literature says engagement is, and perhaps most important, what it is not (c.f., Shuck *et al.*, 2013b for additional information). First, the most common engagement-like states are reviewed, followed by a brief review of more unique engagement states before concluding thoughts are offered.

Work engagement

Work engagement is defined as a positive, fulfilling, work-related state of mind characterized by vigor, dedication, and absorption (Schaufeli *et al.*, 2002). The unique focus of work engagement is toward work and work-based activity.

Work engagement is one of the most researched, well-cited terms in the engagement space to date. To be very specific about what work engagement is, theoretically, the construct has been grounded – and centered – in the burnout literature (e.g., work engagement is the positive antithesis of burnout; Shuck, 2011) and positioned as the antipode to the experience of burnout (Schaufeli *et al.*, 2002). For more complete reviews, see additional resources such as Schaufeli and De Witte (2017) and Schaufeli (2013).

The primary focus of work engagement is work activity that is constructive (i.e., when I get up in the morning, I feel like going to work; Schaufeli *et al.*, 2002), unlike burnout, which, has been defined as a series of work experiences that are destructive. It was Maslach *et al.* (2001) who conceptualized work engagement as the positive antithesis to burnout, when they positioned engagement as "a persistent positive affective state . . . characterized by high levels of activation and pleasure" (p. 417). Here, burnout was theorized to be the result of erosion of engagement (Maslach *et al.*,

2001); work that was once important, meaningful, and challenging became unpleasant, unfulfilling, and meaningless (Maslach *et al.*, 2001, p. 416).

In their early work, the work engagement construct was operationalized simply as the reverse scores on the Maslach Burnout Inventory (MBI-GS; Maslach *et al.*, 1996). It was believed that any employee not experiencing burnout should, theoretically, be engaged with their work. To bring validity to their work, Schaufeli *et al.* (2002) empirically tested the Maslach *et al.* (2001) framework using the MBI-GS (i.e., General Survey), although it was at this time that the use of the definition of engagement changed and shifted theoretical positions. Instead of the seminal *engagement* term used in Maslach's previous publications, Schaufeli *et al.* (2002) began to define engagement as a "positive, fulfilling, work-related state of mind that is characterized by vigor, dedication, and absorption" (p. 74) and renamed the state of engagement, *work engagement*.

While the construct of work engagement has been widely popular, it is not without serious critics. For example, Rich *et al.* (2010) have suggested that items on the UWES "confound engagement with the antecedent conditions suggested by Kahn" (p. 623). Newman and Harrison (2008) have been harsh detractors, proposing that "almost every item from an engagement scale endorsed by Macey and Schneider (i.e., the Utrecht Work Engagement Scale of Schaufeli and Bakker, 2003) is paralleled by a nearly identical item from a well-known measure of job satisfaction, job involvement, positive affect, or organizational commitment" (p. 32). In later works, Newman and colleagues declared the UWES (and with it the idea of engagement) redundant. Saks and Gruman (2014) wrote that "much of the research on engagement is grounded in research on job burnout (Maslach *et al.*, 2001)" and so its distinctiveness could be – and should be – called into question. Saks and others went on to discuss that despite efforts by Schaufeli and colleagues, a core component of the work engagement construct was still considered to be the positive antithesis of burnout and bemoaned the similarities in measurement between the MBI and the UWES (Saks and Gruman, 2014).

In a decisive piece published in the *Journal of Management*, Cole *et al.* (2012) concluded that the sub-dimensions of work engagement and burnout shared highly correlated and similar patterns (they used the word *identical*), which, in their interpretation of the data, indicated that work engagement and burnout shared similar nomological networks and were not independent constructs. In their closing remarks, Cole *et al.* (2012) summed up their position, suggesting, "Researchers interested in advancing contemporary thinking on engagement should avoid treating the UWES as if it were tapping a distinct, independent phenomenon" (p. 1576).

Despite widespread criticism, work engagement remains a very viable and well-used construct. While researchers commonly use employee engagement and work engagement synonymously, the two terms do not mean the same thing. Employee engagement is noticeably different and is reflective of an active psychological state and inclusive of the full spectrum of the immediate working experience (i.e., work, job, team, and the active experience of working), whereas work engagement is limited to only the work and is task driven rather than experience driven. Table 2.2 summarizes some of the main points of difference and theoretical grounding, and directs readers to root citations for deeper reading on the topic.

Job engagement

After Rich *et al.* (2010) declared that items on the UWES confused the construct of engagement with antecedent conditions of engagement, his team developed a new engagement-like construct they called *job engagement*. Where Schaufeli and colleagues took a decidedly divergent approach from Kahn, Rich *et al.* (2010) embraced Kahn's ideals and linked back to the roots of personal engagement, grounding their work in the theoretical propositions of personal engagement, explicitly.

Rich *et al.* (2010) defined job engagement as a "multi-dimensional motivational concept reflecting the simultaneous investment of an individual's physical, cognitive, and emotional energy in active, full work performance" (Rich *et al.*, 2010, p. 619). The unique characteristic of job engagement is, specifically, the focus of energy in active, full work performance toward the *job*.

The focus of job engagement is job activity. Thus, job engagement describes the degree to which a person is engaged with their job only, whereas employee engagement – as detailed earlier – focuses toward the fuller experience of an employee's active role within the experience of their work, including their work, job, team, and organization. This is an important distinction for both scholars and practitioners alike and highlights the unique differences between terms that sound the same yet remain focused toward different outcomes and which develop differently.

In more recent work, scholars reliably narrow the focus of job engagement to the job specifically and do not generalize the term to the work experience, or any general experiences of the working context. For example, Owens *et al.* (2016) positioned job engagement as capturing the level of absorption and dedication an employee has toward his or her job while other researchers continue to conceptualize job engagement as a simultaneous and extensive investment of physical, cognitive, and emotional energies directed to job roles, specifically (Barrick *et al.*, 2015, Rich *et al.*, 2010).

Despite the term *work* in their definition, Rich *et al.* operationalized job engagement through the Job Engagement Scale (JES; Rich *et al.*, 2010), by

Construct Reference Point	Root Citation	Definition and Main Points of Differentiation	Theoretical Grounding and Measurement Tool	Sample Scale Items
Work Engagement	Schaufeli et al. (2002)[1]	Positive, fulfilling, work-related state of mind characterized by vigor, dedication, and absorption	Work activity and work itself as measured by the Utrecht Work Engagement Scale (UWES) or UWES-9	When I get up in the morning, I feel like going to work. To me my job is challenging.
Burnout	Maslach and Jackson (1981)	A syndrome of emotional exhaustion, depersonalization, and reduced personal accomplishment that can occur among individuals who do people work of some kind	Burnout as a disease state of exhaustion and cynicism and lack of personal accomplishment as measured by the Maslach Burnout Inventory General Survey (MBI-GS)	I feel emotionally drained from my work. I doubt the significance of my work.
Psychological Engagement	May et al. (2004)	Harnessing of organizational members' selves to their work roles; in engagement, people employ and express themselves physically, cognitively, and emotionally during role performances (Kahn, 1990)	The psychological conditions of engagement (i.e., meaningfulness, safety, and availability) originally proposed by Kahn (1990) measured by the Psychological Engagement Scale	The work I do on this job is very important to me. I am confident in my ability to display the appropriate emotions at work.
Job Engagement	Rich et al. (2010)	Multi-dimensional motivational concept reflecting the simultaneous investment of an individual's physical, cognitive, and emotional energy in active, full work performance	Job activity as measured by the Job Engagement Scale (JES)	I work with intensity on my job. I am excited about my job.

(Continued)

Table 2.2 (Continued)

Construct Reference Point	Root Citation	Definition and Main Points of Differentiation	Theoretical Grounding and Measurement Tool	Sample Scale Items
Intellectual, Social, Affective Engagement	Soane *et al.* (2012)	The extent to which one is intellectually absorbed in work, experiences a state of positive affect relating to one's work role, is socially connected to the working environment, and shares common values with colleagues	Work activity and alignment with colleagues as measured by the Intellectual, Social, Affective Scale of Engagement (ISA)	I share the same work values as my colleagues. I am enthusiastic about my work.
Employee Engagement	Shuck *et al.* (2017c)	Active, work-related positive psychological state operationalized by the intensity and direction of cognitive, emotional, and behavioral energy	Active role and full spectrum expression of the working experience as measured by the Employee Engagement Scale (EES)	I feel a strong sense of belonging to my job. I give my job responsibility a lot of attention. I am willing to put in extra effort without being asked.

asking participants a series of questions that required a keen focus on their job framework (i.e., I work with intensity on *my job* and I am excited about *my job* [italics added for emphasis]). Notwithstanding use in the field, no definition of job engagement indicated this narrow focus, nor was there a more general descriptor of how job engagement should be defined beyond the context of the job. Indeed, beyond Rich *et al.*'s work, job engagement is far less used in the research literature than terms such as employee engagement and work engagement, respectively, but this is likely a function of a still maturing idea over a duplication of ideas.

What may seem interesting about the development of the job engagement construct is the influence of Schaufeli and colleagues' research on work engagement and the overlap. For example, as noted in their work on job engagement, Owens *et al.* (2016) wrote about absorption and dedication, two of the main ideas of work engagement, but cross-referenced with job engagement. More, research by Lauring and Selmer (2015) reported that the physical dimension of job engagement is often described as feeling vigorous while cognitive engagement could be described as absorption. Notwithstanding, the elements of engagement noted by Schaufeli and colleagues have been distinctly defined as work engagement, which should be, and is, different from job engagement (for emperical details of this distinction, see Nimon *et al.*, 2016a).

While employee engagement has a rooted, historical development, job engagement does not yet enjoy a theoretically grounded record. As of the writing of this book, scholars have neglected the theoretical development of the job engagement construct. For example, while we can point to literature that speaks to the ideas of maintenance, intensity, and direction of employee engagement, no such theoretical lineage exists yet for job engagement. It is often used as a passthrough term, or as an antecedent to some organizational performance idea, but in its present state lacks definition and theoretical context.

Emergent engagement types in the literature

Social engagement

Similar to the JES (Rich *et al.*, 2010), the condition-oriented ISA construct (intellectual, social, and affective engagement; Soane *et al.*, 2012) is focused toward social engagement, an often overlooked and relational component of the engagement experience (Kahn and Heaphy, 2014). In a departure from traditional engagement-type states, Soane and colleagues proposed that engagement had a collective social aspect, a decidedly innovative application (see Soane *et al.*, 2012, for additional details). Grounded in the work of Jackson *et al.* (2006), Soane *et al.* (2012) proposed the idea that engagement was a collective experience, shared among others in the formation of that experience, and this experience had a social component. Some work, especially work by Owens *et al.* (2016), has looked more deeply into the relational nature of engagement by offering a new scale of relational energy.

Connected to the core ideas presented by Soane *et al.* (2012), the ways in which employees interacted with their social environment (i.e., colleagues, peers, other stakeholders) likely impacted the experience of engagement at work. Across the research literature, however, very little work has compared social engagement and employee engagement; however, employee engagement, while encompassing how people experience and respond to their co-workers, is also focused on a host of other important areas (as previously noted) and seems unique in conceptualization (Saks and Gruman, 2014; Saks, 2006; Saks, 2008; Shuck and Reio, 2014) from social engagement as presented by Soane *et al.* (2012).

More research is needed in this area, but the rigorous research by Katie Baily and her colleagues in the UK (i.e., Alfes, Soane, Shantz, and Fletcher) provides a promising new avenue of inquiry around the application of employee engagement that looks to extend the concept into more human dimensions and applications of work in the coming decade.

Organizational engagement

Organizational engagement was a term coined by Saks, who in his later writing was hyper-critical of the employee engagement term (Saks, 2008; Saks and Gruman, 2014). Saks defined organizational engagement in some of his very early work as "the extent to which an individual is psychologically present in a particular organizational role" (Saks, 2006, p. 604), focused toward organizational identification.

Employee engagement and organizational engagement sound similar yet are different constructs altogether. For example, organizational engagement is operationalized as how *captivating* and *exhilarating* a person experiences their organization (c.f., Saks, 2006 [italics appear in the original]) while employee engagement is inclusive of an attachment-like state but is not specifically bound by it (Shuck et al., 2017a). Employee engagement is more broad-based and holistic of the employee experience, whereas organizational engagement is much more focused on a connection – or pledge – to the organization as an entity.

Beyond work by Saks, the organizational engagement construct has received little attention in recent years, and Saks has migrated his own language over to the term employee engagement (see, for example, Saks and Gruman, 2014; Saks, 2019).

Collective organizational engagement

Using a wider, more group-level scope of organizational engagement, Barrick *et al.* (2015) introduced the idea of collective organizational engagement (COE). COE was defined as "shared perceptions of organizational members that members of the organization are, as a whole, physically, cognitively and emotionally invested in their work" (p. 8). This is an emerging perspective of engagement that is social in nature and that captures the collective conscious of a grouping of employees who are either engaged or disengaged.

Collective organizational engagement was developed using a foundation of well-established theoretical models such as resource management theory and the jobs demands-resource model to show how a collective energy of engagement can influence firm performance. Across the research, COE has been applied in limited fashion and when it has been applied, it has been in support of empirical work using different perspectives (i.e., ISA Engagement; cf. Bailey *et al.*, 2015; Bailey *et al.*, 2017; Soane *et al.*, 2012). While Barrick *et al.* detailed their methodological approach, collective organizational engagement has yet to build a breadth of research in the literature, although, it shows great promise as both a methodology and application for influencing higher levels of employee engagement at the organizational level, in particular when it is applied to firm performance.

While COE is promising, it is also decidedly different from employee engagement most notably in the level of perspective at which it is applied. At present, collective organizational engagement is concerned with engagement at the macro level, where employee engagement is concerned with the individual experience. There is likely overlap between the two, as individual experiences often collate into movements, though no work has connected the two.

Concluding thoughts

As we look back over the literature, it seems clear that the term *employee engagement* is not a substitute for work engagement, job engagement, organizational engagement, intellectual/social engagement, or even collective organizational engagement, although we can see and appreciate the connections that, at times, overlap. Being precise in language and meaning, as well as definition is critical to understanding just what employee engagement is. Differences between terms, their focus, and those nuances impact conceptualization as well as utility and should be noted between scholars and practitioners, alike.

In the next chapter, the expression of engagement is detailed, starting with the antecedents of meaningfulness, safety, and availability and overviewing the connection between cognitive, emotional, and behavioral engagement by way of Kahn's early work.

Note

1 In their article, Schaufeli *et al.* (2002) originally used the term *engagement* to refer to what they later called *work engagement*.

3   The expression of employee engagement

What is employee engagement and how does it feel? Can leaders see it, and how do they know that employees are engaged or not engaged when they are at work? How do we know when we need more engagement, or less? Perhaps most importantly, how does it develop in practice and what can leaders do about it?

The research literature on employee engagement has been historically vague on how engagement develops. Indeed, much of the research has generally assumed that engagement exists and that when it is present, it is has the ability to influence outcomes that have some meaning for organizations. For a variable that presents as so important and critical to business success, perhaps more attention is needed to better explore how engagement develops in real life and what that expression might look and feel like to an individual.

This chapter explores how the expression of engagement might develop and is integrated into work experiences including Kahn's early work on meaningfulness, safety, and availability, more emergent theories that define engagement as a tri-part focus, the role of pride and belief through inward emotional experiences (Shuck and Rose, 2013), as well as the notion of intention versus outcome when it comes to behavioral engagement.

An overview of the expression of employee engagement

Before diving head first into how scholars have positioned the formation of employee engagement, it would be prudent to note that very few researchers have explored the formation of employee engagement in any form. Most engagement scholars assume that the experience is a generally positive one, and while that may be true, most of what we know about engagement could be assumption. The few scholars who have examined the formation of engagement have routinely and overwhelmingly defined engagement as a three-part psychological experience (Kahn, 1990; Harter *et al.*, 2002; May *et al.*, 2004; Saks, 2006; Rich, 2006; Macey and Schneider, 2008; Shuck and Wollard, 2010; Rich *et al.*, 2010; Zigarmi and Nimon, 2011; Wefald *et al.*, 2011; Truss *et al.*, 2013b; Soane *et al.*, 2013; Truss *et al.*, 2013a; Leiter and Maslach, 2017; Schaufeli and De Witte, 2017; Fletcher *et al.*, 2017; Yalabik *et al.*, 2017; Young *et al.*, 2018; Kim *et al.*, 2013; Carasco-Saul *et al.*, 2015).

Kahn (1990) discussed this tri-part experience in his earliest work and Rich *et al.* (2010) pointed to engagement as a cognitive, emotional, and physical experience. Even like constructs such as work engagement speak of engagement occurring as a tri-part phenomenon – although very differently than employee engagement (i.e., vigor, dedication, and absorption). Employee engagement as we have defined it is unique to the individual and grounded in interpretations of an environment that is personally interpreted. According to the research literature, this interpretation occurs by way of how an employee *thinks* about their work, *feels* about their work, and ultimately, intends to *behave* through their work.

In addition to engagement being operationalized as a tri-part psychological experience, scholars have suggested that employee engagement is a latent phenomenon. That is, you cannot see an employee cognitively or emotionally engage, and leaders cannot physically touch high levels of engagement, but there are observational indicators when engagement is present. Employees might be able to sense when they are really engaged, and leaders may very well be able to see high levels of engagement manifested through higher levels of performance, yet the actual construct does not physically manifest as behavior because it is a psychological experience. In its final and most complete form, engagement is an intention to behave but is not yet the behavior (Shuck *et al.*, 2017a; Shuck and Wollard, 2010; James *et al.*, 2011; Shuck *et al.*, 2011a).

Employees routinely bring a full range of cognitive, emotional, and physical energies to their work roles that express the full experience of what it means to be engaged (Kahn, 1990). When it comes to employee engagement, Shuck *et al.* (2017a) and Shuck and Wollard (2010) both proposed that experiences of cognition and emotion were significant and critical expressions of the engagement experience. In their comprehensive overview of employee engagement, Shuck *et al.* (2017c) noted that expressions of cognition and emotion were a kind of *psychological appraisal* connected to the meaningfulness, safety, and resource availability of lived and future-expected experiences of work, similarly to how Kahn had positioned personal engagement in his early work. These experiences – or moments – are utilized in the development of mental and emotional representations that inform final decision making. An appraisal is defined as an individual, psychological assessment regarding the impact of the current environment connected to future behavior (Lazarus, 1984; Lazarus, 1982; Nimon and Zigarmi, 2014). Tzeng

(1975) suggested that appraisals about work or otherwise occur within a system's framework that considers multiple perspectives of information simultaneously.

Only a handful of scholars have examined the elements of cognition and emotion that make up the general focal point of engagement in practice (Xanthopoulou *et al.*, 2012). Even smaller numbers of scholars have examined cognitive, emotional, and physical energies as separate sub-concepts or facets, leaving an important aspect of the formation of employee engagement underdeveloped (see Shuck *et al.*, 2017c for more details). For detailed reviews of the latent formation of employee engagement, see Saks and Gruman (2014), Shuck *et al.* (2017a), Shuck *et al.* (2014), Shuck and Wollard (2010), and Soane *et al.* (2012).

In the next sections, the literature across the spectrum of employee engagement research is considered in an attempt bridge both historical and emerging engagement theory. For example, Kahn's work in its pure form has been covered in great detail (see Chapter 2), and now, that theory (i.e., Kahn's theory of personal engagement) is integrated alongside more contemporary and emerging work as a way to connect the theoretical spectrum. Kahn's work stands alone, as does Rich *et al.* (2010), Shuck *et al.* (2017c), and Saks (2006). This chapter is not meant to supplant their influential work, but rather investigate potential connections between the theory and practice as well as connect the dots between literature bases. This chapter is a narrative exploration of the expression of engagement as detailed throughout the pattern of literature across the academic landscape.

Cognitive engagement

When an employee is cognitively engaged, they are mentally and psychologically involved with the task at hand – maintaining intensity and direction toward completion. Cognitive engagement has been defined as the degree and intensity of mental energy that an employee contributes toward positive organizational outcomes (Rich, 2006; Rich *et al.*, 2010; Shuck *et al.*, 2015; Shuck and Reio, 2014; Kahn, 1990).

Cognitively engaged employees are attentive and concentrated in their workplace, and they distribute the full spectrum of mental energy toward work-related activities. Building from Kahn's (1990) early work, cognitive engagement is characterized by the ways in which an employee directs cognition in both direction and proportion – illustrated by an employee's expression of focus and attention as well as concentration toward work-related tasks, experiences, and contexts. Connected to historical engagement theory, levels of cognitive engagement might originate from an employee's appraisal of whether their work is or was meaningful and safe (physically, emotionally, and psychologically), and whether or not they believe they have sufficient levels of resources to complete their work. The proportion of each informs the experience of cognitive engagement at basic, driving levels (Porath and Pearson, 2012; Shuck *et al.*, 2017c; Saks and Gruman, 2014), but at a minimum, is connected to the cognitive appraisal process at play when employee engagement is expressed in practice.

The meaningfulness appraisal

Meaningfulness is defined as the positive "sense of return on investments of self in role performance" (Kahn, 1990). Conceptual and empirical research has demonstrated the naturalistic need employees have for growth, generativity, and purpose toward experienced meaningfulness in their work and life (Barrick *et al.*, 2013; Zigarmi *et al.*, 2011; Grant, 2008; Oldham, 2012; Fairlie, 2011). This need for meaning is absolutely central to the role of personal involvement and personal investment that human beings are drawn towards throughout fulfillment of their overall life roles (cf. Maslow, 1968). Kahn (1990) suggested that when individuals believed their actions were meaningful, both to the individual as well as to the acted upon context or object, they would choose to engage in proportionate degree. Otherwise, leaders could expect some level of disengagement or non-engagement with employees who beleived their work was meaningless or unsafe.

The meaningfulness variable completed a circular model where employees believed they added value and significance to the work they are doing as well as received feedback about their value and significance to an organization (Maslow, 1970; Kahn, 1990).

The safety appraisal

Employees routinely make cognitive appraisals regarding the perceived safety of their current environment. Safety in the context of engagement is defined as the ability to show one's self "without fear or negative consequences to self-image, status, or career" (Kahn, 1990).

Safety revolves primarily around each employee's need to trust their working environment cognitively, emotionally, and behaviorally, as well as the need to reasonably understand what is expected of them at work (i.e., job descriptions, contingency plans, feedback from a supervisor, etc.). The degree to which an employee believes their environment is safe and that engaging in an activity, taking on a new challenge, or working with a team of colleagues will offer a degree of relative security and protection, they are likely to engage mentally at proportionate levels.

The availability appraisal

The availability appraisal, perhaps more than any other, highlights the convergence of cognitive capacity in an employee's personal and professional life. Availability is defined as the "sense of possessing the physical, emotional, and psychological resources necessary" (Kahn, 1990) to complete one's work.

Practically, availability revolves around whether or not employees feel they have the tools to complete their work or that at a minimum, these tools are within reach and obtainable. Tangibly, the availability of resources might be understood as items such as supplies, sufficient budget, and manpower to complete a task (Harter *et al.*, 2010; Wagner and Harter, 2006; Harter *et al.*, 2002). Intangibly, the availability of resources could be understood as opportunities for learning and skill development (Czarnowsky, 2008), a reasonable degree of job fit (Resick *et al.*, 2007), and commitment to the organization (Meyer *et al.*, 2010; Meyer and Allen, 1997).

Interestingly, while the two domains of personal and professional resources often remain in separate domains by function and location – particularly within the fields of human resources and management, the availability of resources can pull each employee in competing and at times conflicting cognitive directions. For example, an employee who is asked to stay late at work to finish a project (i.e., to be engaged in their work) might pull resources from his or her personal life (e.g., spending time with family, going to the gym, volunteering at a church, or meeting friends for dinner).

In summation, when an employee cognitively assesses whether or not a situation or context is meaningful, safe, and resource sufficient, that appraisal is used to determine overall significance of a situation, serving as the catalyst toward full engagement. Meaningfulness, safety, and resources act interdependently from one another, yet are symbiotically linked as experiences that inform one another as engagement develops. This interpretation reflects a level of engagement, or movement, toward their work (Brown and Leigh, 1996; Kahn and Heaphy, 2014; Kahn, 2010; Fairlie, 2011; May *et al.*, 2004).

A brief exploration of the research on meaning, safety, and availability

To be clear, Kahn did not connect his findings with experiences of cognitive, emotional, and behavioral engagement. Indeed, he did not even use those words. Yet, over the past decade, contemporary engagement scholars (Saks, 2019; Fletcher *et al.*, 2017; Shuck *et al.*, 2017c; Bailey *et al.*, 2017; Joo *et al.*, 2017) have explored unique interpretations of Kahn's work, as a way to fuse his early work with an emerging understanding of the phenomenon. Several scholars have, for example, undertaken exploratory research that has laid the early groundwork for how scholars and practitioners can better understand the expression of engagement in both theory and practice.

For example, one of the first studies to explore Kahn's (1990) conceptualization of engagement suggested that all three conditions were critical to the development of employee engagement (May *et al.*, 2004). Using a sample of 203 employees from a large insurance firm, results indicated that engagement had a positive relation to meaningfulness ($r = .63$), availability ($r = .29$), and safety ($r = .45$). After 2002, use of Kahn's conceptualization, while widely cited as foundational scaffolding, was scarcely used in framework development until more recent applications.

Rich *et al.* (2010) expanded the research around these three domains, showing that engagement (his term was *job engagement*, see Chapter 2 for more information on the JES), as manifested through meaningfulness, safety, and availability, mediated the relation between value congruence, perceived organizational support, core self-evaluation, and two outcome variables, task performance and organizational citizenship behavior. Important here was the connection of Kahn's research to the emerging tri-part framework of employee engagement we know today. Shuck *et al.* (2011a) provided evidence that job fit, affective commitment, and psychological climate were all significantly related to employee engagement and that employee engagement was significantly related to discretionary effort and intention to turnover. More precisely, affective commitment, meaningfulness, and availability, as measured by the May *et al.* (2004) scale, were unique predictors of intention to turnover ($\beta = -.21$, $p < .001$, $\beta = -.19$, $p < .05$) connecting, in exploratory fashion, some of Kahn's conditions to direct experiences.

More recent research has looked deeply into the role of meaningfulness, safety, and availability as an application to practice. For example, Fletcher *et al.* (2017) utilized a unique multi-level diary methodology to explore the psychological conditions of engagement. Their work suggested that meaningfulness and availability mediated perceptions of a working context and engagement. They contextualized engagement by positioning these three psychological conditions as antecedents in the engagement process (Cole *et al.*, 2012; Kahn, 1990; Rich *et al.*, 2010; Saks and Gruman, 2014). Hernandez and Guarana (2018) added additional evidence using a conditional-indirect effect model, which highlighted the role of these three psychological conditions on outcomes of engagement. Hernandez and Guarana (2018) concluded that "engagement is not only affected by employees' contemporaneous understandings of their jobs but also influenced by their perceptions of anticipated opportunities" (p. 1711). This might be defined as a cognitive appraisal, or in emerging terms, cognitive engagement.

Concluding thoughts on cognitive engagement

A host of research has explored cognitive engagement and its relation to outcomes such as organizational and financial accomplishment (Salanova *et al.*, 2005), lower turnover intention (Shuck *et al.*, 2011a; Alarcon and Edwards, 2011; Lu *et al.*, 2016), lower absenteeism and shrinkage (Harter *et al.*, 2010), more in-role and extra-role behavior (Bakker and Schaufeli, 2008), higher organizational commitment (Schaufeli and Bakker, 2004), and wellbeing (Joo *et al.*, 2017), among others. In summation, cognitively engaged employees would answer positively to statements such as "The work I do makes a contribution to the organization," "I feel safe at work; no one will make fun of me here," and "I have the resources to do my job at the level expected of me."

It is important to note that in Kahn's original work, the psychological conditions detailed were meant to collectively lead to the "holistic" experience of engagement not just one form of engagement, yet when integrated across the spectrum of engagement theory, these conditions are *so critical* and *so powerful* that they are positioned as the primary evaluative component of any context or situation related to work. The degree of meaningfulness, safety, and resource availability that an employee perceives defines the proportionality of engagement an employee is willing to cognitively engage with, which then leads to emotional and behavioral engagement. This is not meant to be limiting or context binding, but rather, context defining in scope and until more research is undertaken, theoretical in nature.

Emotional engagement

Emotional engagement revolves around the broadening and investment of the emotional resources an employee has within their influence. In the research literature, emotion is often referred to, and used synonymously, with the term *affect* (see, for example, Tzeng, 1975; Zajonc, 1980; Lazarus, 1982; Porath and Pearson, 2012; Shuck and Reio, 2014; Mahon *et al.*, 2014).

Once a context or situation is appraised as being meaningful, safe to engage with, and as having adequate resources (i.e., the employee has a sense of cognitive engagement), employees develop valuation appraisals regarding their current environment that are emotional in nature. The sub-dimension of emotional engagement is the deliberate offering of resources to a situation, person, or context directionally proportionate to the degree of meaningfulness, safety, and availability evaluated in any one situation. When a situation is meaningful, an employee might give of their time or invest in learning a new skill, for example.

Employees routinely and reliably direct the resources they have influence over such as time, knowledge, pride, belief, and attention as an artifact of valuation when choosing to emotionally engage in their current environment. The investment of resources may seem trivial at first; however, consider the work of a pride-filled employee who fully trusts their work environment. The positive emotions of pride and trust stem from cognitive appraisals made about the environment during the previous stage (e.g., cognitive engagement; this work is meaningful, it is safe for me here at work, and I have the resources to complete my tasks). Here, cognition and affect have a shared relation (Fugate *et al.*, 2011) and, perhaps, more fully express Kahn's original intention. The mental schema formed within the cognitive evaluation process serves as a primary appraisal that drives and directs emotion toward a target into a holistic, full expression of engagement.

This proportionate offering is supported by research in similar domains through theories of reciprocity (Černe *et al.*, 2014) and social exchange (O'Boyle *et al.*, 2012).

Concluding thoughts on emotional engagement

Pride, belief, and *accomplishment* are powerful motivational states that pull forward. In the context of work, an employee might show up for work fully engaged when they are full of pride, believe their work matters, and that their accomplishments are valued. In the research literature, *pride, belief,* and *accomplishment* are identified as currencies of contextual value that drive emotional engagement and that are connected back to Kahn's original work on personal engagement (Shuck and Rose, 2013).

Emotional appraisals of engagement are in constant flux, dependent on continuous monitoring of cognitive cues (e.g., the ebb and flow of meaningful, safe, and resource-full experiences). Within this process, it is important to note that cognition and emotion are bi-directional and codependent with each other, as well as an expression of holistic engagement. Indeed, each appraisal relies on the other, developing toward purposeful and intentional work behavior that is meaningful, safe, and resource sufficient, as well as intentional (Barrick *et al.*, 2013; Barrick *et al.*, 2015).

Behavioral engagement

As a final focal point to the expression of employee engagement, behavioral engagement is the most overt form of the employee engagement process. It is often what we can see someone do. The sub-dimension of behavioral engagement is defined as the psychological state of intention to behave in a manner that positively impacts performance (Macey and Schneider, 2008; Rich *et al.*, 2010). Tangibly, behaviorally engaged employees are believed to be willing to put in extra effort, work harder for their team and organization, and to do more than is expected – among a host of other variables. In their seminal model, Macey and Schneider (2008) referred to this state of engagement as proactive engagement – because it was a forward moving, psychological state which manifested as behavior – but was not yet materialized in action. This remains an important and distinguishing factor in the employee engagement literature.

Understood as the physical manifestation of cognitive and emotional engagement, behavioral engagement can be understood as increased levels of effort directed toward organizational goals (Macey and Schneider, 2008; Shuck and Wollard, 2010). Behavioral engagement represents a psychological state that is not yet action-related behavior (which, differentiates it from performance, or other related constructs such as organizational citizenship behavior, which is the actual behavior) but is connected to expressions of cognition and emotion (Kahn, 1990; Shuck *et al.*, 2017c). It is not enough to just work harder; behaviorally engaged employees see themselves as psychologically *willing* to give more and going above and beyond in a way that characterizes their forward expression and movement.

Put a different way, behavioral engagement is the expansion of an employee's available resources displayed overtly in the form of an intention. From this context, employee effort in the context of engagement is linked to intentions related to increased individual effort. While many scholars agree that being an engaged employee includes at least some element of cognition and emotion, few agree on its physical manifestation. Unfortunately, this has contributed to spurious claims of redundancy and to the misconception of defining employee engagement as an observable outcome (e.g., organizational citizenship behaviors, discretionary effort, actual turnover, working faster; Harrison *et al.*, 2006; Newman and Harrison, 2008; Newman *et al.*, 2011).

Engagement cannot be both a state and an observable behavior (Schaufeli, 2013). Those two conceptualizations are different. While intention and behavior may co-occur – and even co-exist – they cannot co-materialize simultaneously as the same thing (Shuck *et al.*, 2017c). Behavioral outcomes (i.e., what some scholars refer to as behavioral engagement; cf.

Macey and Schneider, 2008; Saks, 2008) occur only after a psychologically grounded intention to act is formed (Zigarmi and Nimon, 2011; Nimon *et al.*, 2011) through expressions of cognitive and emotional engagement. Actual, observable behavior such as effort, creativity, and turnover must be distinguished from the intention to put in effort, the intention to be creative, and the intention to voluntarily leave an organization. Employee engagement concerns a forward moving intention of energy, but it is not the physical, observable behavior of that manifestation (Parker and Griffin, 2011).

Post-behavior, the employee engagement process does not remain static; the cycle is in constant monitoring, where information regarding behavioral contexts resulting from the expression of being engaged are monitored, and socioemotional and physical environmental feedback are looped into newly forming cognitive appraisals that ascribe a continuous flow of meaning and value that drive expressions of emotional engagement (Shuck *et al.*, 2017c; Shuck *et al.*, 2017a). This process continues through a cumulative building and a reciprocal process, which guides the lived experience of an employee being engaged. Employees who are behaviorally engaged answer positively to statements such as "When I work, I intend to push myself beyond what is expected of me" and "I plan to work harder than is expected to help my organization be successful."

Concluding thoughts

Many scholars and practitioners make the mistake of only looking at observable behavior when they define or attempt to measure engagement. Behavior is certainly one way of looking at engagement, but often what we see someone do is a lag measure to what they are thinking about and feeling in the moment. Perhaps a more holistic approach would be to consider the full expression of engagement by digging more deeply into how employees are thinking about the meaning and safety of their working experience, feeling about that context, and intending to be in their workspace as well as how those experiences are connected back to what we theorize and know about employee engagement.

Certainly, the expression of employee engagement can seem complex and this chapter, unlike the other chapters throughout this book, is admittedly more theoretical in scope. Latent constructs can be difficult to measure and a challenge to track because we cannot see them. This is especially true when marrying theory to practice. More, finding ways to honor historical theory alongside the blending of contemporary thinking can be a delicate balance, and this chapter has attempted to do just that by overviewing the full spectrum of research in a way that respects and credits foundational scaffolding as scholars build sophistication into an under-standing of an expression we cannot easily observe.

Certainly, cognition and emotional appraisals, intention, and interpretation can all sound quite complicated. To be more accessible, we might consider a model that simply says employee engagement is the way in which employ-ees *think about, feel about*, and ultimately *intend* to *do their work*, every day. The think, feel, do model of employee engagement, while simple, is sup-ported by decades of detailed research – historical and contemporary – that explores how each expression makes up the experience of being engaged.

In the next chapter, emerging trends in employee engagement research are detailed, starting with an identification of measurement tools, followed by a juxtaposition of employee engagement alongside job satisfaction, job commitment, job involvement, and the role of affect in the engagement experience.

4 Emerging developments in employee engagement research

Employee engagement has been one of the highest trending topics in the management and human resource literature over the past 20 years. More than 82,000 articles and research reports on employee engagement have been written from 2010 to present day. Over the past few decades, scholars have shown fierce interest in two important and emerging developments: *measurement* and *overlap*.

Within each area, the research literature has been ripe with opinions and ideas about how to best measure employee engagement as well as how and when employee engagement is related to other well-known constructs, such as job satisfaction and organizational commitment. Understanding how to best examine engagement, as well as knowing how engagement connects to a broader, bigger picture of organizational performance is helpful as scholars and practitioners make choices about utility, worth, and effectiveness.

In the following sections, how employee engagement has been examined and measured in the research literature is explored as well as what emerging tools are gaining traction in publication. Measurement has certainly been an important topic of legitimizing the engagement construct over the course of its development, and there are, at times, differing opinions. Second, this chapter explores the notion of construct overlap and how engagement is different and similar from other well-established ideas throughout the management and human resource literature.

Exploring and measuring employee engagement

There exist many recorded ways to examine employee engagement. Several scholars, many who are mentioned throughout this book, have offered their own unique lean on how best to explore and measure engagement. Overwhelmingly, the literature on employee engagement has been dominated by quantitative approaches, but early qualitative work led the way for under-standing the concept as we know it today. This chapter is broadly focused on the most classic approaches as well as the emerging tools demonstrated by their use in the research literature. Because qualitative research has been the foundation for the theoretical development of the construct, a brief over-view of qualitative work is positioned as the precursor to the later emerg-ing quantitative methodologies. Exploratory approaches and measurement tools that were mentioned only a handful of times, or that were rough varia-tions of classic methods were not included in this chapter; instead, only the most widely used as well as most promising applications of exploring and measuring employee engagement are detailed.

In the research literature, the term *employee engagement* is rather new relative to other organizationally focused terms like *satisfaction* and *com-mitment*. Because of this, measuring engagement has taken many forms and fallen under different umbrella terms. To be as inclusive as possible, this chapter covers the breadth of measurement tools that have been used to measure *engagement*, including those that fall under terms like *work engagement*, *job engagement*, and *psychological engagement* as a way to broaden the theoretical network of engagement into practice. Leaving these tools out would be problematic and short-sighted, as so much of the history and future of employee engagement is intertwined with like ideas and constructs.

As a helpful tool for scholars and practitioners, a summary table is pro-vided that matches each measurement tool to a root citation, grounded con-ceptual framework, and sample scale items. Most of the tools covered are available for use in academic work, but it is recommended that interested scholars and researchers reach out to primary authors to gain permission for use.

Qualitative approaches to exploring employee engagement

Only a handful of studies have explored employee engagement using a qualita-tive approach yet some of the most foundational work has been qualitatively focused. For example, the methodology in Kahn's (1990) seminal work on personal engagement can at times be overshadowed by its seminal standing in the field. As detailed previously, Kahn used an ethnographic-grounded theory approach to detail his unfolding understanding of engagement – a study that many scholars point to as one of the first published research articles on the topic.

One of the more robust and early qualitative approaches to exploring engagement was offered by Jones *et al.* (2011), who – similar to Kahn

(1990) – also used an ethnographic approach to capture the essence and individual experience of engagement in the United Kingdom. The Jones *et al.* (2011) model proposed a "life cycle of engagement" and underscored the challenges and opportunities of public service workers' engagement. This research was some of the first to look at a cycle of engagement, and at the time of their writing, represented only a handful of scholars who were using a deeply qualitative approach to better understand what employee engagement was and how it was experienced on the ground level. Connected, as an extension of their earlier work, using an auto-ethnographic approach, Jones (2012) detailed the pressures and inconsistencies between organizational interventions and personal levels of engagement through narrative story telling. This work highlighted the manifestation of the engagement experience as a pseudo-application of the Job Demands-Resources model, as well as how pressure works to enhance or detract from the engagement experience. Related, Shuck *et al.* (2011c) employed a single case study methodology to examine the experiences of work with food service employees at a large multinational service corporation. Their work proposed an emergent model of engagement and provided a descriptive framework of engagement from which to build Human Resource Development-related interventions.

In more recent research, reflective work by Fletcher has continued the stream of innovative and deeply individual qualitative research. In his work on personal role engagement, Fletcher (2017) interviewed 124 employees (N = 1,446 situational observations) from six UK organizations about their experiences with the emotional, cognitive, and physical aspects of personal role engagement. Findings suggested that there existed levels of variation in task and personal resources. Fletcher's study was one of the first to explore the everyday experiences of engagement and one of the only more recent qualitative approaches in the literature. For more detailed information, see Fletcher *et al.* (2017), Fletcher (2016a), and Fletcher (2016b).

As evidenced by the brevity of this section, there is perhaps an under-reliance on qualitative work, as so much of the documented research in human resource and management journals is overwhelmingly survey focused (Bailey *et al.*, 2017). In the sections that follow, the classic quantitative approaches are detailed, followed by more contemporary measurement approaches.

Classic quantitative approaches to employee engagement

Utrecht work engagement scale

The Utrecht Work Engagement Scale (UWES) has been by far the most widely utilized scale for measuring work engagement in the world and is often used in research as a proxy for employee engagement (see, for example, de Villiers and Stander, 2011; Diedericks and Rothmann, 2013). To be clear, the UWES measures work engagement, not employee engagement, but prior to 2017, there was not an established measure for employee engagement in the field, and as a stand-in, scholars frequently used the UWES as a best-case substitution.

Developed by Wilmar Schaufeli, a distinguished and preeminent scholar in the occupational health and human resource fields, the UWES was designed to theoretically align with the definition and theoretical grounding of the term work engagement. Work engagement was defined as a "positive, fulfilling, work-related state of mind that is characterized by vigor, dedication, and absorption" (Schaufeli *et al.*, 2002, p. 74). There are two well-established versions of the UWES – a 17-item scale and a shorter, 9-item scale.

The long version of the UWES (i.e., the UWES-17) was first published in 2002 and the short version (i.e., the UWES-9) published in 2006 (Schaufeli *et al.*, 2006). Both scales included separate subscales for the focal constructs: *vigor*, *dedication*, and *absorption*. These three focal constructs were characterized as high levels of energy, a sense of significance, and the perception of being fully engrossed in one's work. Engagement, as measured by the UWES (Schaufeli and Bakker, 2003), was theorized to be the polar opposite of burnout in work. This was evidenced by earlier work that positioned work engagement as the reverse of scores on the Maslach Burnout Inventory-General Survey 1986 (Maslach *et al.*, 1986), which was also a three-factor scale (e.g., *exhaustion, cynicism,* and *ineffectiveness*).

In their very early work, Schaufeli *et al.* (2002) detailed the construct validity for the UWES-17, including confirmation of the three-factor structure (e.g., *vigor, dedication,* and *absorption*), which provided appropriate and acceptable levels of reliability and discriminant validity from the MBI-GS's exhaustion and cynicism factors, a critical theoretical distinction. In later work, Schaufeli *et al.* (2006) also published evidence of construct validity for the UWES-9, including confirmation of the three-factor structure across ten international samples, moderate levels of reliability, and excellent levels of convergent validity with the original longer scales. See Table 2.2 for reference points, root citations, and sample scale items.

Maslach Burnout Inventory General Survey

Very few contemporary scholars have continued use of the Maslach Burnout Inventory General Survey (MBI-GS) as a proxy for engagement, however, because the UWES is so popular and so connected to the to the MBI, it is worth noting. The MBI-GS, developed by Maslach and Jackson (1981), considered burnout to be a chronic disease state of wariness. In comparing the two scales, Schaufeli *et al.* (2002) noted that the MBI-GS differs from the MBI in that the former does not reference the other people with whom one is working – a critical point of context for understanding work engagement.

In parallel to the theoretical framework of burnout, the MBI-GS contains separate scales for *exhaustion, cynicism,* and *professional efficacy*. Maslach and Jackson (1981) explained that the exhaustion domain measured fatigue, cynicism reflected indifference, and the professional efficacy of both social and nonsocial aspects of occupational accomplishments. While high scores on exhaustion and cynicism and low scores on professional efficacy are indicative of *burnout* low scores on exhaustion and cynicism, and high scores on efficacy were believed to be suggestive of *engagement*.

The conceptual and empirical overlaps of both of the UWES and the MBI-GS have been problematic in the literature. Several scholars have cautioned the simultaneous use of both the UWES and the MBI-GS, and provided conceptual and empirical reaction to the use of engagement and burnout when engagement (work, employee, or job) is operationalized using the UWES (interested readers are encouraged to see Cole *et al.*, 2012 for more detailed information on this discussion). See Table 2.2 for reference points, root citations, and sample scale items.

Psychological engagement scale

May *et al.* (2004) attempted to construct an empirical measure of Kahn's original personal engagement construct, using the three distinct dimensions of cognitive, emotional, and physical engagement as well as an examination of the conditions of engagement proposed by Kahn (1990). May *et al.* (2004) proposed six unique scales of varying length. Cognitive engagement was measured by a 4-item scale; emotional engagement measured by a 5-item scale; physical engagement measured by a 5-item scale; meaningfulness measured by a 6-item scale; safety measured by a 3-item scale; and finally, availability measured by a 5-item scale.

Items were purposefully designed to "reflect each of the three components of Kahn's (1990) psychological engagement" (May *et al.*, 2004, pp. 20–21) and to capture the unique, individual experience of full engagement (cognitive, emotional, and physical). The subscales were comprised of questions that reflected an individual employee's perception of their working context. Well-grounded in the literature, empirically, the scales did not hold up psychometrically as hoped, failing to show any empirical distinction between the constructs (e.g., meaningfulness, safety, and availability). Finding that the scale reported acceptable levels of reliability when modeled as a single factor, May *et al.* (2004) collapsed the meaningfulness, safety, and available scales together as a specific measure of *full psychological engagement*. The cognitive, emotional, and physical engagement scales were collapsed into a single engagement measure, but the collapsed scale showed little promise for measuring employee engagement or the experience of engagement that Kahn's work had alluded toward.

The Psychological Engagement Scale (May *et al.*, 2004) has very limited use in the research literature. Nonetheless, the scale is noteworthy as one of the first and perhaps only attempts at quantifying Kahn's notion of personal psychological engagement. A few researchers have refined the Psychological Engagement Scale (c.f., Shuck *et al.*, 2011a) and repurposed the scale as a proxy measure of employee engagement, but at present the scale remains dormant. See Table 2.2 for reference points, root citations, and sample scale items.

Contemporary quantitative approaches to employee engagement

Job engagement scale

Somewhat similar to May *et al.* (2004), the Job Engagement Scale (JES) was developed by Rich *et al.* (2010) to conceptualize Kahn's (1990) personal engagement construct refocused more toward the context of work. The JES is an 18-item instrument that includes three distinct scales: *cognitive engagement, emotional engagement*, and *physical engagement*. The cognitive engagement scale was based on Rothbard's (2001) early measure of engagement and considered both levels of attention and absorption, which mapped theoretically to the UWES (Schaufeli and Bakker, 2003) absorption scale. The emotional engagement scale was based on Russell and Barrett's (1999; Barrett and Russell, 1999) collective research on *core affect* and focused on emotions that reflected the combination of high pleasantness and high activation as well as emotions related to work. This subscale concentrated on the emotion of pleasantness and high activation as they related to experiences of in-work perceptions of the environment. The physical engagement scale was based on Brown and Leigh's (1996) measure of work intensity, defined as "energy exerted per unit of time" (p. 362).

Initial evidence suggested that the JES fit a higher-order factor structure where the three first-order factors loaded onto a second-order factor with moderate levels of reliability (Rich *et al.*, 2010). Factor loadings and individual scale items were all positive, strong, and statistically significant.

Rich *et al.* (2010) suggested that his scale sufficiently supported Kahn's conceptualization of engagement.

As alluded to in Chapter 2, the JES was offered as a specific deviation from Schaufeli's work and the UWES. Rich *et al.* (2010) gently suggested that many of the items on the UWES simply failed to capture the full range of psychological experiences connected to engagement as reported by Kahn and thus developed the JES. The unique focal point of the JES is on energy in active, full work performance toward a job. Despite the term *work* in the definition (see Chapter 2), throughout the JES (Rich *et al.*, 2010), participants are asked to respond to a series of statements that require them to focus toward a job context (i.e., I work with intensity on *my job*, and I am excited about *my job* [italics added for emphasis]). See Table 2.2 for reference points, root citations, and sample scale items.

The Intellectual Social Affective Scale of engagement

One of the more emerging and exciting areas of development related to the measurement of engagement is the Intellectual Social Affective Scale (ISA; Soane *et al.*, 2012). The ISA is a 9-item scale designed to reflect a work-role focus, activation, and positive affect regarding the extent to which one is intellectually absorbed in work, experiences a state of positive affect relating to one's work role, and is socially connected and shares common values with colleagues.

The more condition-oriented ISA construct (intellectual, social, and affective engagement; Soane *et al.*, 2012) is focused toward social engagement, an often overlooked and relational component of the engagement experience (Kahn and Heaphy, 2014). Published recently in 2012, use in the field is growing and the ISA is becoming a broadly used tool for measuring engagement grounded in Kahn's (1990) original conceptualization, especially in the UK. Psychometrics of the ISA were developed across multiple studies, lending considerable credibility to the tools reported construct validity, scale structure, and association to important outcomes such as intention to turnover, task performance, and organizational citizenship behavior. See Table 2.2 for reference points, root citations, and sample scale items.

The Employee Engagement Scale

The Employee Engagement Scale was developed to align theoretically and conceptually with the Shuck *et al.* (2017c) definition of employee engagement. Shuck *et al.* defined engagement as an active, work-related positive psychological state (Macey and Schneider, 2008; Shuck and Wollard, 2010; Rich *et al.*, 2010; Christian *et al.*, 2011; Parker and Griffin, 2011; Saks and Gruman, 2014; Kahn and Heaphy, 2014; Nimon *et al.*, 2016b; Fletcher *et al.*, 2017; Yalabik *et al.*, 2017) operationalized by the intensity and direction of cognitive, emotional, and behavioral energy (Shuck and Wollard, 2010; Saks and Gruman, 2014; Kahn, 2010; Kahn, 1990; Rich *et al.*, 2010). The EES is a 12-item, 3-dimensional measurement tool designed to reflect the degree and proposition of cognitive, emotional, and behavioral energy that an employee maintains in intensity toward their work.

In their positioning, Shuck *et al.* explained that an employee's investment of cognitive, affective, and behavioral energies was believed to be a distinct, work-related positive, psychological experience (Shuck *et al.*, 2014). The sub-dimension of cognitive engagement was defined as the intensity of mental energy expressed toward positive organizational outcomes (Rich *et al.*, 2010; Shuck *et al.*, 2017a; Shuck *et al.*, 2017b; Shuck *et al.*, 2017c; Joo *et al.*, 2017). Emotional engagement was defined as an employee's intensity and willingness to invest emotionality toward positive organizational outcomes (Macey and Schneider, 2008; Shuck *et al.*, 2017c; Shuck *et al.*, 2017a; Joo *et al.*, 2017). Behavioral engagement was defined as the psychological state of intention to behave in a manner that positively impacts performance (Macey and Schneider, 2008; Rich *et al.*, 2010).

Shuck and colleagues developed the EES across four independent studies, using each to build the next step in the measurement protocol. Across the first two studies, the EES was found to consist of three sub-factors (cognitive, emotional, and behavioral) and a higher-order factor (employee engagement). More specifically, the researchers explored the factor structure and reliability of the EES (Study 1), then refined the scale, confirmed the factor structure, and examined reliability and both convergent and nomological validity evidence (Study 2). In Study 3, the authors completed a final reduction in scale items and examined additional evidence of reliability and nomological validity as well as evidence of discriminant validity, and Study 4 was designed to test for evidence of incremental validity. See Shuck *et al.* (2017a) for more details.

The EES is arguably one of the most emergent tools for measuring employee engagement, specifically. At present, it remains the only tool available designed specifically to measure the psychological state of employee engagement – not job engagement (JES: Rich *et al.*, 2010; Crawford *et al.*, 2010; Saks, 2006), work engagement (UWES; Schaufeli *et al.*, 2006; Hallberg and Schaufeli, 2006; Bakker *et al.*, 2008; Schaufeli, 2013; Schaufeli and De Witte, 2017), organizational engagement (Saks,

2006), or intellectual and/or social engagement (Soane *et al.*, 2012). See Table 2.2 for reference points, root citations, and sample scale items.

Employee engagement and job attitude overlap

Within the literature, serious – and at times, well-grounded – debate has called into question the conceptual and empirical worth of the employee engagement construct. Scholars have questioned whether or not employee engagement provided anything new or whether engagement was just a clever repackaging of ideas.

This question of worth has been a point of division in some literature circles, especially when employee engagement is compared (and used) alongside work-related constructs like *job satisfaction, organizational commitment*, and *job involvement*. These three job attitudes seem to be the focus of the most critique when it comes to employee engagement. Specifically, questions have surfaced – on multiple occasions – about whether employee engagement is redundant with the previously conceptualized *A*-factor (Newman and Harrison, 2008; Newman *et al.*, 2010, Newman *et al.*, 2011). The *A*-factor, an idea proposed by Harrison *et al.* (2006), is a grouping of three "classic job variables" (i.e., job satisfaction, organizational commitment, and job involvement; Newman *et al.*, 2010) believed to encompass a higher-order attitudinal factor. According to Newman, the *A*-factor is a general job attitude combined of the unique variance attributable to job satisfaction, organizational commitment, and job involvement. That is, the *A*-factor is the sum of the parts for job satisfaction, job involvement, and organizational commitment.

Newman argued emphatically that these three classically situated constructs (e.g., job satisfaction, organizational commitment, and job involvement) substantially overlapped with each other and "exhibit[ed] important theoretical and empirical redundancy" (p. 46) with employee engagement. Alongside the *A*-factor, Newman and colleagues (2010) also proposed an *E*-factor, a multidimensional, behaviorally based construct composed of various outcome-based performance variables such as citizenship behaviors and withdrawal activities (i.e., absence, turnover, etc.). By way of numerous works, Newman *et al.* (2010) demonstrated that the *A*-factor was related to the *E*-factor ($r = .50$). Using the UWES as a secondary measure of engagement, Newman *et al.* (2011) later asserted that attitudinal engagement was the *A*-factor and that engagement appeared to be superfluous. To be more specific, according to Newman and colleagues, "measures of attitudinal engagement appear[ed] to reflect the *A*-factor" (p. 40) thus positioning the emergent construct of employee engagement as completely redundant, theoretically and empirically.

Claims by Newman *et al*. were supported in the field through other empirical offerings. For example, Cole *et al*. (2012) offered a definitive piece suggesting that engagement was overlapping, and redundant with burnout (using the UWES as a measure, and work engagement as the focal construct). They wrote, "The most frequently used inventory of employee engagement (viz., UWES) is shown to be empirically redundant with a long-established, widely employed measure of job burnout (viz., MBI)" (p. 1576). Other scholars have critiqued engagement conceptually, suggesting that engagement represents corporate exploitation and a political tool used to re-norm the cult of overwork, including a reframing of reasonable working conditions.

Despite compelling evidence from some scholars of overlap, research has equally pointed towards distinction. In one example, Shuck *et al*. (2016b) decomposed the variance of two separate measures of engagement side-by-side (i.e., the UWES-9 and the Job Engagement Scale) alongside the three commonly compared job attitudes. Their results suggested that no first-order, second-order, or third-order commonality coefficients fully explained, either standalone or in combination, all the variance in the two separate measures of engagement. Such findings continue to be well aligned and supported by previously established research (c.f., Schaufeli *et al*., 2002).

Several scholars have also conceptually explored the overlap of engagement with job attitudes and like constructs (Albrecht, 2010; Newman *et al*., 2010; Nimon *et al*., 2016a; Saks, 2008; Saks and Gruman, 2014; Shuck *et al*., 2013b; Shuck *et al*., 2016b; Shuck *et al*., 2017c; Yalabik *et al*., 2017). In the following sections, the literature on engagement and each focal job attitude is explored in brief detail and constructs juxtaposed alongside one another as a means to lay out the evidence. First job satisfaction and engagement are explored, followed by organizational commitment and job involvement. The final section examines the role of affect, or emotion, alongside engagement and explores potential implications for practice when affect is considered a component within or overlapping alongside employee engagement.

Employee engagement and job satisfaction

Employee engagement and job satisfaction are frequently linked in the research literature. Both seem "cut from the same cloth" (Shuck *et al*., 2017c, p. 5) as the two are linked in theory, research, and practice and at times, measurement. Theoretically speaking, job satisfaction may very well develop under similar conditions of engagement, and in this regard, job satisfaction has been conceptualized as a job attitude (Newman *et al*., 2011). Job attitudes have been known to co-occur within components of other attitudes (intra-component satisfaction) or alongside components of other attitudes such as job involvement, organizational commitment, and employee engagement (inter-component satisfaction) (Shuck *et al.*, 2017a).

In the research literature, the focus of job satisfaction has primarily served as an evaluative context. This evaluation is developed from conditional summary statements concerning the job (e.g., I am satisfied with my work). Job satisfaction has been defined in the literature as a valuation of satiation "resulting from the appraisal of one's job or job experiences," and as stationary (Locke, 1976, p. 1300). The positioning has represented a very different and unique positioning from the definitions of employee engagement offered by a host of scholars.

Satisfaction has most frequently been referred to as a global, general, work-related perception focused toward a state of satiation (Nimon *et al.*, 2016a). Certainly, employee engagement and job satisfaction are likely associated, in that employees who are highly engaged may also be satisfied. Job satisfaction has often, however, been focused most frequently toward the job level, as a temporal, general indicator of employee sentiment that is static rather than forward moving (Brief and Weiss, 2002). That is, satisfaction may reflect an employee who is satisfied in general but may not also be actively motivated (Macey and Schneider, 2008). An employee could be satisfied about their current conditions and not motivated to do anything more about them. This is the core of satisfaction and the differentiator from employee engagement.

In distinguishing satisfaction and engagement, scholars have contrasted conceptual and empirical distinctions between static descriptions of satisfaction and active descriptions of engagement (Xanthopoulou *et al.*, 2012; Cooper Thomas *et al.*, 2010) suggesting job satisfaction (when defined as satiation rather than confounding the construct with affect) is largely grounded in statements of an individual's sense of fulfillment with, and through, aspects of the general working environment. This positions job satisfaction as an indicator of fulfillment rather than a motivational psychological experience (Yalabik *et al.*, 2013). Employee engagement, on the other hand, is represented by an active psychological state. As noted previously, employee engagement is notably different as engagement manifests itself as an active, motivational state contextualized by the psychological interpretation of the working experience.

Employee engagement and organizational commitment

Similar to job satisfaction, organizational commitment and employee engagement share characteristics of overlap and redundancy. Scholars often refer to organizational commitment as the far more affect-related construct, which has inadvertently positioned employee engagement more closely to affective organizational commitment as opposed to normative or continuance commitment (Gruman and Saks, 2011; Guest, 2014).

Within the vast fields of literature, researchers have routinely suggested that engagement contains a component of commitment embedded within the construct (Macey and Schneider, 2008; Shuck *et al.*, 2013a). For example, when employees are highly engaged, they are far more likely to report higher levels of organizational commitment. As a distinguishing nuance between the two, however, researchers have positioned organizational commitment as "the relative strength of an individual's identification with and involvement in a particular organization" (Mowday *et al.*, 1979, p. 226). While often used in research as a focal perspective of work (e.g., how *committed* an employee is), organizational commitment is an outcome of engagement, not a unique focal perspective of the work experience itself (Shuck and Reio, 2014; Owen *et al.*, 2014).

More specifically, the degree to which employees are organizationally committed is representative of their relative attachment to the organization. Organizational commitment is a function of something that happens to an employee not through an employee. That is, they become affectively committed or attached. Organizational commitment, then, represents a pledge to act in some way toward the organization resultant of attachment, which is a function of the engagement experience and is not an indicator of sentiment toward the working experience itself. On the other hand, while employee engagement describes an active motivational state that is non-static, and forward moving, organizational commitment is positioned as the outcome of that engaging experience.

While distinguished conceptually in the literature, employee engagement and organizational commitment also share a common set of antecedents and consequences. Examples include perceived organizational support, supportive organizational culture, and leadership (Lok and Crawford, 1999; Rhoades *et al.*, 2001; Wollard and Shuck, 2011). Consequences include but are not limited to organizational citizenship behavior, turnover intent, and performance (Brown, 1996; Meyer and Allen, 1997; Meyer *et al.*, 2002; Riketta and Landerer, 2002).

Conceptually and empirically, employee engagement may be associated with higher levels of commitment, especially affective commitment – a cycle that is likely to be self-fulfilling over time (Shuck *et al.*, 2017c; Shuck *et al.*, 2017a) – but the constructs remain decidedly distinct in contextual positioning as antecedent and outcome. It is likely that organizational commitment and employee engagement are mentalized differently yet practically co-occur simultaneously in experience.

Employee engagement and job involvement

Clear parallels can be made between both employee engagement and job involvement, especially when considering the focus of job involvement toward different attentions in application. Job involvement is defined as "the degree to which a person is identified psychologically with his work, or the importance of work in his total self-image" (Lodahl and Kejnar, 1965, p. 24), yet the literature has been less clear about positional distinction. For example, using a meta-analytic approach to examine the construct of job involvement, Brown (1996) suggested, "[Job] involvement implies a positive and relatively complete state of engagement [regarding the] core aspects of the job itself" (p. 235) and according to Macey and Schneider (2008), job involvement occupied the same conceptual space of engagement. On the other hand, job involvement has been positioned as ego involvement (Lawler and Hall, 1970; Vroom, 1962) and conceptualized as an identity-related construct (Kühnel *et al.*, 2009), whereas employee engagement was believed to be a motivational psychological state (Kahn, 2010; Kahn, 1992; Kahn, 1990).

Notwithstanding, the distinctive conceptual positioning of job involvement is supported throughout the research in theoretical propositions advocated by Shuck *et al.* (2013b) and research by Shuck *et al.* (2014) suggesting that job involvement and employee engagement were tied primarily at the cognitive level, only. For example, May *et al.* (2004) suggested, "Engagement may be thought of as an antecedent to job involvement in that individuals who experience deep engagement in their roles should come to identify with their jobs" (p. 12). Further, Saks (2006) argued that job involvement was a cognitive judgment about the job itself, which was tied to self-image, where employee engagement was a broader, more inclusive construct consisting of energy and enthusiasm toward the job (Christian *et al.*, 2011; Rich *et al.*, 2010).

Macey and Schneider (2008) further posited that engagement and job involvement likely shared some level of construct overlap, citing definitions that specifically mentioned facets of employee engagement linked with job involvement. Scrima *et al.* (2013) demonstrated this distinction empirically. In their work, job involvement and engagement (as well as affective commitment) were differentiated conceptually in both focus and feature, and engagement fully mediated the relationship between job involvement and affective commitment (Scrima *et al.*, 2013).

Unlike job involvement, engagement is not only identity focused, but is a present-focused state looking toward the future. While engaged employees may be likely to identify with their role in work, the limiting capacity of job involvement as a primarily cognitive function is suggestive of distinction between the two.

Similar to job satisfaction, both job involvement and employee engagement have a propensity to share common antecedents such as esteem, supervisory support, and feedback as well as to be related to common organizational outcome variables such as performance and employee turnover (Brown, 1996; Brown and Starkey, 2000; Brown and Leigh, 1996), which is perhaps why the two are commonly used together. A comparison of the definitions of the two constructs, however, helps make clear that the focus of job involvement is toward cognition – a kind of pledge (Lawler and Hall, 1970; Lodahl and Kejnar, 1965; Kanungo, 1982; Paullay *et al.*, 1994), whereas, engagement, according to most definitions (Saks and Gruman, 2014; Saks, 2006; Shuck and Wollard, 2010; Shuck *et al.*, 2016b; Shuck *et al.*, 2017c; Shuck *et al.*, 2017b; Shuck *et al.*, 2017a; May *et al.*, 2004; Frank *et al.*, 2004; Richman, 2006; Rich *et al.*, 2010; Crawford *et al.*, 2010), encompasses three dimensions of experience: cognition, emotion, and behavior.

Employee engagement and emotion

A wide range of scholars have suggested that engagement has a component of emotion embedded within the core experience – including some of the earliest work by Kahn as well as scholars on the leading edge of engagement research such as Soane, Fletcher, Bailey, Schaufeli, Bakker, Shuck, and Nimon. Several have even gone so far as to position emotional engagement as a definitive component of the employee engagement experience. Clearly, engagement and emotion are related, but how?

One of the first steps in understanding the relationship between engagement and emotion lies in defining what we mean when we use the term *attitude*. If engagement is emotion, emotion must be a type of attitude, and engagement has been reliably positioned as an attitude. An attitude is defined as "a psychological tendency . . . expressed by evaluating a particular entity with some degree of favor or disfavor" (Eagly and Chaiken, 1993, p. 1). Within the broader line of research on attitudes, Hulin and Judge (2003) suggested, "the original tripartite definition of attitudes comprising cognitive, affective and behavioral elements has [been] eroded in industrial and organizational (I/O) psychology until we are left with assessments of attitudes as cognitive evaluations of social objects" (p. 256). Other authors (Brief and Weiss, 2002; Zajonc, 1980) have noted an emphasis toward favoring cognitive approaches to the formation of an attitude (i.e., job involvement). Because of the nature and definition of the concept of attitudes, all attitudes should have something in common, no matter what particular entity might be evaluated (be it a job, work, the organization, etc.). This is, perhaps, what Newman was arguing for in presenting the *A*-factor. In agreement with other scholars (Eagly and Chaiken, 1993; Thoresen *et al.*, 2003; Kuppens *et al.*, 2013; Binneweis and Fetzer, 2010), all attitudes – including job satisfaction, organizational commitment, job involvement, and employee engagement – are understood to have a sense of affect (valence and intensity), which, makes up an outward expression.

Throughout the research literature, the concept of attitude presumes a dimension of affect and cognition in an evaluation, which assigns a degree of positivity or negativity to an object (Eagly and Chaiken, 1993). All attitudes have this affective dimension in common (Thoresen *et al.*, 2003). The presence of affect within an attitude does not make the cognitive content of various related attitudes redundant, or more importantly, unworthy as some scholars have suggested. Evaluation of an object can be cognitive and affective although affective responses are more than evaluations and not all evaluative judgments are purely affective (Hulin and Judge, 2003; Zajonc, 1980). When attitudes have different foci, they may also have different origins and end points, and therefore require different approaches including measurement, which might be suppressed when lumping them together under a central theme – or higher order factor.

While an employee might show similar disfavor (or favor) in their affective attitudes towards the organization and/or to their job simultaneously, the resulting attitudes are different, as they would refer to different foci, each with different cognitive and affective qualities as well as intensities and directions dependent on psychological conditions.

When it comes to understanding employee engagement, scholars have been definitive that an important dimension of the engagement experience is emotional. Indeed, Shuck *et al.* (2014) suggested that of the three sub-factors of engagement (cognitive, emotional, and behavioral), emotional engagement was most predictive when it came to behavior connected to performance. Emotion and engagement are interwoven experiences in many ways, yet they remain distinct in their functions. Employee engagement is a type of attitude where emotion (or affect) is an appraisal that has valence and intensity, yet when embedded within employee engagement, directs the maintenance, intensity, and direction of energy (Shuck *et al.*, 2017a).

Concluding thoughts

There is a voluminous record of research on employee engagement. Reams of articles and opinions have been written, yet so much of what has been offered continues to cover similar conceptual spacing. Engagement is routinely measured using one of three tools (i.e., the UWES, JES, or EES), and scholars continue to debate the uniqueness of engagement alongside well-documented and historical constructs like job satisfaction, job involvement, and organizational commitment, and to discuss whether or not engagement and affect are related, the same, or redundant. These debates are tried and true and will likely continue long after this book is published. However, the research seems to be gaining clarity.

Employee engagement is not job satisfaction, job involvement, or organizational commitment. All four are unique and interesting constructs that have long and storied historical roots throughout the research literature. Within the framework provided in this book, the UWES measures work engagement, the JES measures job engagement, and the EES measures employee engagement. Alongside these tools, new and interesting measurement conceptualizations are taking shape, including qualitative methodologies that dig into the lived and expressed experiences of engagement and which are still developing in practice.

This chapter has attempted to summarize the overarching perspectives of these arguments, present emerging empirical methodologies and ways of looking at employee engagement, as well as detail the ongoing conversation. These discussions are certainly interesting, yet the allure of engagement is perhaps, first and foremost, grounded in the impact higher levels of engagement have on individuals and organizations.

The next chapter examines this very impact, starting with the impact of employee engagement on organizational performance indicators, and then details the impact of high (and low) levels of engagement on the individual, concluding with a brief summary of why engagement could matter to leaders in small and large organizations, alike.

5   The impact of employee engagement

In 1999, Marcus Buckingham and Curt Coffman authored a book that put the subject of employee engagement at center stage. It featured, in great detail, results from a longitudinal Gallup study about the impact that employee engagement can have on a business. The popularity of the book, *First, Break All the Rules* (Buckingham and Coffman, 1999), helped the term "employee engagement" become an overnight sensation. Soon after, professional societies and international consulting groups (e.g., The Gallup Organization, BI WORLDWIDE, CIPD, Mercer, the Corporate Leadership Council, ASTD, and SHRM) quickly staked claim to expertise in the employee engagement arena. As these groups have encouraged companies to survey, pulse, and listen to the employee voice, and follow the value proposition of their workforce, the mantra of employee engagement has reached fever interest far and wide.

The literature on employee engagement is overflowing with compelling narratives around the hefty impact of engagement. The outcomes of employee engagement are advocated to be exactly what most leaders seem to need today: employees who are more productive, profitable, safer, healthier, creative, less likely to turnover, less likely to be absent, more likely to engage in organizational citizenship and helping behavior, and more willing to engage in discretionary efforts (Sheridan, 2017; Potgieter, 2016; Wildermuth, 2008; Czarnowsky, 2008; Lockwood, 2007; Arakawa and Greenberg, 2007; Wagner and Harter, 2006). Further, engaged employees average higher customer satisfaction ratings and generate increased revenue (Vance, 2006; Wagner and Harter, 2006), and early evidence is suggestive of a direct employee engagement-profit linkage (Czarnowsky, 2008; Ketter, 2008; Harter *et al.*, 2010). It is not surprising that corporate executives are consistently ranking the development of an engaged workforce as an organizational priority. If engagement can produce all of this, what leader would not want their employees to be engaged?

Before diving into the literature on the outcomes and impact of employee engagement, we should address two compelling issues regarding the current state of the research on engagement. First, much of the scholarship on engagement – at least up to this point – has focused exclusively on the outcomes of engagement at the expense of theoretical, definitional, and even conceptual development. So, while leaders want more engagement, very few know what they are asking for when they want employees to be engaged. This has resulted in an objectification of the construct, which has, at least in some areas of practice, removed the employee from employee engagement, resulting in a confusing state of affairs. This is especially true in books like *Employee Engagement for Dummies* (Kelleher, 2013), or when consultants refer to employees as "prisoners" (Hewitt, 2015). In other words, when a leader wants more engagement, they may look for "easy steps" (Lockwood, 2007) or "top ten" lists (Potgieter, 2016), which give very little insight into how engagement develops. As long as employees are moving faster, making more money, and coming up with better ideas, how it happens can be of little concern. This book has taken the opposite approach. Instead of focusing first on just the outcomes, we started with an understanding of the principles that influence praxis – how engagement is defined, expressed, and measured – and only now focus toward impact and outcomes. The hope is that this principle-based approach will help advanced practitioners in human resources, leaders of organizational divisions, and executives make grounded, evidence-based decisions that influence the outcomes of employee engagement in an everyday manner without objectifying and stretching the construct beyond its intended use. Engagement will not solve all of your problems, yet, reading the literature without a critical lens, it might be tempting to believe that employee engagement is a magic bullet and that it is exceedingly easy to develop. It is not.

This brings us to the second major issue. Despite loads of research, much of what has been written about the linkages between employee engagement and performance is grounded in research that could be interpreted as subjective, often cross-sectional, and grounded very little in solid evidence-based practice (Briner, 2015). Take for example the recent narrative analysis by Bailey *et al.* (2017). Their excellent research noted important empirical linkages between employee engagement and variables such as job satisfaction, organizational commitment, and intention to turnover, as well as in-role, extra-role, and counter-role behaviors. To be clear, their results were promising and insightful and their methodology rigorous by any standard. Bailey *et al.* (2017), however, contended that much of the existing research included in their study was restricted and incomplete, often grounded in cross-sectional, self-report measures, potentially confounded by common methods bias, with almost no evidence of replication. Here is a team of highly respected scholars, taking the issue of employee engagement head on, and the best they can offer is that, "given the scarcity of studies, their individualistic nature, methodological limitations and the range of interventions studied, it is difficult to draw any robust conclusions" (Bailey *et al.*, 2017, p. 44). Taking a far more extreme perspective, Briner (2014) suggested that research on employee engagement is contaminated with over-hyped claims, widespread misunderstanding, and inaccurate measurement.

Because of these two issues – the objectification of employee engagement and the scarcity of robust, evidence-based practice from which leaders can draw– perhaps, the literature on employee engagement is reflecting a critical turn. For example, some have suggested the development of engagement as a murmuration of objects (Keenoy, 2013), a political, social, academic, and consultancy of objects and clever marketing tricks that benefit the corporate machine at the expense of the employee (i.e., the outcome perspective). Guest (2014) has routinely positioned the construct of engagement as the exploitation of individual agency that manipulates the reality of modern work. Valentin (2014) argued that engagement might not actually exist at all, but rather represents corporate propaganda and a deceitful discourse, stressing that for some, engagement was a socially constructed, altered, skewed, and invented reality of work. In other words, employee engagement was make-believe. Engagement has also been positioned as "fabricated through discourse, staged through performance, and fictionalized through text" (Ybema *et al.*, 2009), and still others have voiced serious doubt about the overly romantic outlook of engagement as a quantifiable experience altogether (e.g., Newman *et al.*, 2011; Griffin *et al.*, 2008; Pugh *et al.*, 2008; Newman and Harrison, 2008; Saks, 2008; Hirschfeld and Thomas, 2008). Perhaps, this is due in large part to so much of the research on engagement being focused acutely toward outcomes without any theoretical, definitional, or measurement context, and, which has throughout the literature streams on engagement, taken for granted critical assumptions about the expression, control, and influence of engagement. When scholars have focused exclusively on outcomes, and when engagement is devoid of the employee, as Wagner (2015) put it, employees are used as resources to be manipulated and controlled, in the same way that lumber, coffee beans, and cattle are resources to be categorized, catalogued, and measured.

Any conversation about the impact and outcomes of employee engagement should note these challenges, and readers should be aware that they exist. Engagement cannot be polyenoic. Any serious endeavor into understanding the employee engagement context should be overlaid with the reality of what engagement is and how it can be best deployed in practice. With this in mind, throughout the following sections, this chapter overviews the documented impact of employee engagement, starting with a look into organizational impact, followed by the individual impact, and concluding with an emerging and potentially exciting subsection of research around health and health outcomes related to the experience of engagement. So much research has been written on employee engagement that it would be impossible to cover every article in this short-form book. Instead, each section provides an overview with citations so that interested readers can go further if they choose, and then dives into a handful of seminal and current research to bring depth and contour to the deployment, utilization, and understanding of the impact and outcomes related to higher levels of employee engagement.

ORGANIZATIONAL IMPACT

It is, perhaps, the potential for organizational impact that is most exciting for leaders when it comes to employee engagement. Leaders at all levels have been captivated by the connection between higher levels of engagement and a host of organizationally focused outcomes. For example, employees who have reported heightened levels of employee engagement also report lower levels of turnover (Maslach *et al.*, 2001; Saks, 2006; Saks and Gruman, 2014; Shuck and Reio, 2014; Shuck *et al.*, 2013a) and higher levels of job performance, task performance, organizational citizenship behaviors (Rich *et al.*, 2010), productivity (Christian *et al.*, 2011; Richman, 2006), discretionary effort, affective commitment, positive psychological climate (Wollard and Shuck, 2011; Shuck *et al.*, 2011a), job satisfaction, continuance commitment (Saks, 2006), customer service (Rurkkhum and Bartlett, 2012), and customer-rated employee performance and customer loyalty (Salanova *et al.*, 2005). As if this were not enough evidence of organizational benefit, heightened levels of employee engagement have been further associated with increased profitability, revenue generation, and strategic growth (Xanthopoulou *et al.*, 2009). Indeed, the research literature is overflowing with scholarship pointing to the positive potential impact of employee engagement.

So far, throughout this text, we have paid particular attention to the development of engagement, its definition, and measurement. However, there are additional scholars whose work has shaped the field, especially around the potential for engagement to have an impact. We start first with seminal work by Harter *et al.* (2002) and Saks (2006), and detail several other scholars' work, concluding with Barrick *et al.* (2015).

If it was Buckingham and Coffman that popularized employee engagement in the practitioner literature, it was their fellow colleagues from Gallup that did the same for the academic literature. Post Kahn's (1990) seminal work on personal engagement, the idea of engagement laid inactive for nearly a decade. Very little work was undertaken that had engagement as the core focus. In 2002, Harter *et al.* published one of the earliest and most definitive pieces of literature on employee engagement in the *Journal of Applied Psychology*. Using the same framework popularized by Buckingham and Coffman (1999) – which was introduced by the late visionary Donald O. Clifton in 1985 as a part of the Gallup Strengths movement – Harter and colleagues (2002) pulled data from a sample of 7,939 business units across multiple industries to examine the impact of engagement on business unit performance.

The results of their meta-analysis showed that organizational culture should, and could, be measured at the individual level by looking at separate business units, separate unit managers, and separate unit employees. Using the Gallup Work Audit (GWA), a proprietary 12-item questionnaire (Buckingham and Coffman, 1999), results suggested that employee engagement had a positive relation to important business outcomes such as customer satisfaction (r^1 = .33), turnover (r = −.36), safety (r = −.32), productivity (r = .20), and profitability (r = .17). Harter *et al.* (2002) further suggested that companies who scored .43 standard deviations above the median on the composite GWA enjoyed higher levels of overall performance (i.e., an average of a 103% higher success rate at the business unit level) than those on the lower end of the median. Results of their research suggested that while the study indicated only moderate effect sizes, such modest evidence often translated into significant practical results for an organization's profitability. In later works (Harter *et al.*, 2003; Fleming and Asplund, 2007; Wagner and Harter, 2006), Gallup researchers claimed that engagement developed one micro-culture at a time, highlighting the individual psychological perspective of engagement and contending that engagement is local first, then global. In later updates, Gallup researchers continued to drive scholarship from the practitioner perspective with a growing database of 10 million participants speaking 51 languages from 736 organizations in 144 different countries.

While Harter *et al.*'s article was a landmark for the engagement field, their work is scarcely used at present date. This is perhaps due in part to the proprietary nature of the Gallup Q_{12} and the challenges that independent researchers have in accessing the tool. The Harter *et al.* (2002) study is noteworthy as a demonstrated part of the historical record of employee engagement and associated outcomes. For more detailed information about the work by Harter *et al.* interested readers should see Harter *et al.* (2002) and Harter *et al.* (2010).

Saks' work on the outcomes of engagement has been a flagship resource scholars have looked toward for more than two decades. Saks (2006) was one of the first to suggest that employee engagement – as a term – was best understood through the social exchange framework and the first to separate *job engagement* and *organizational engagement* under the umbrella of employee engagement (c.f., Saks, 2006 for specific definitions and conceptual framework). Saks was quick to propose a three-component model (cognitive, emotional, and behavioral engagement), which was well aligned with much of the work already covered throughout this book (e.g., Kahn, 1990; Maslow, 1968; Maslow, 1970; Maslach *et al.*, 2001; Harter *et al.*, 2002).

Noting that employee engagement was quickly becoming a trending topic, Saks put his three-component model to the test following in the academic footsteps of work by Baumruk (2004), Harter *et al.* (2002), and Richman (2006), who had all detailed linkages between engagement and organizational outcomes. Results indicated that engagement was related to job satisfaction ($r = .26$), organizational commitment ($r = .17$), and intention to quit ($r = -.22$).

Christian *et al.* (2011) completed, at the time of their writing, the most comprehensive meta-analytic review of engagement outcomes to date. The primary purpose of their work was to distinguish engagement from other like constructs, and to explore the theoretical merit of the engagement construct. Due to the amount of data collected, Christian *et al.* were able to report on a host of antecedents and outcomes related to engagement, offering a broad picture of the construct using results from 770 effect sizes[2] (a population of 91 studies, 80 of which were published).

In terms of outcomes, Christian *et al.* reported that engagement was related to job satisfaction ($M\rho = .53$), organizational commitment ($M\rho = .59$), job involvement ($M\rho = .52$), task performance ($M\rho = .43$) and contextual performance ($M\rho = .34$). Work by Christian *et al.* (2011) paralleled that of Rich *et al.* (2010) who offered compelling evidenced of the relationship between engagement and task performance ($M\rho = .25$) and organizational citizenship behaviors ($M\rho = .27$). In addition to the work by Christian *et al.* (2011), Cole *et al.* (2012) undertook their own meta-analytic look at engagement. Their work was decidedly focused on construct proliferation and redundancy (see Chapter 3) and only sparsely reported outcomes. Interested readers are encouraged to look more closely at Christian *et al.* and Cole *et al.* to get a full perspective of the engagement construct from their viewpoints.

More recently, Bailey *et al.* (2015) explored the outcomes of engagement through a narrative analysis – a rigorous, systematic review of the evidence of engagement to date. In total, Bailey *et al.* (2015) examined 214 studies focused on the meaning, antecedents, and outcomes of engagement. Their methodology was robust and likely the most ardent attempt at exploring the evidence-based practice of employee engagement to date. In their work, Bailey, Madden, Alfes, Fletcher, *et al.* reported that employee engagement was found to be positively associated with individual morale, knowledge sharing, innovation, task performance, extra-role performance, and organizational performance. Results showed that "engagement was most strongly correlated with job satisfaction ($M\rho$ = 0.57) and organizational commitment ($M\rho$ = 0.52). There was also a moderate correlation between engagement and turnover intentions (−0.38), in-role (0.36), extra-role (0.36) and counterproductive ($M\rho$ = −0.32) performance" (Bailey *et al.*, 2015, p. 43). For additional work by this author team, interested readers should see Bailey *et al.* (2017), Truss *et al.* (2013b), and Truss *et al.* (2013a).

Finally, through an interesting application of employee engagement theory, Barrick *et al.* (2015) offered some of the most compelling research to date about the connection between employee engagement and firm performance. Barrick *et al.* were focused on data from a larger research study that promoted best leadership practices in financial institutions (small credit unions were used in their sample). Their results were clear. Engagement was shown to significantly and positively affect firm performance. Indeed, Barrick *et al.* went òn to suggest that engagement was "the only variable among [their] predictors, moderator, and control variable that had a significant direct relationship with firm-level performance" (p. 122). This was in line with pervious work that had suggested a connection between financial returns and higher levels of employee engagement (Xanthopoulou *et al.*, 2009). Xanthopoulou *et al.* (2009) examined a much smaller, yet significant sample of employees working in three branches of a fast-food company. Results from their exploratory study highlighted the impact of coaching with day-level work engagement, which was shown to influence financial returns, on both the day of the coaching as well as the next days' financial returns.

Throughout this section, we have explored only a fraction of the research, yet the connection between engagement and a host of organizationally focused outcomes seem to be gaining clarity. There is at least an association between employee engagement and performance on many levels, and the organizations that are able to develop and influence environments that foster engagement are likely to benefit from a host of positive outcomes, including everything from innovative behaviors and higher levels of commitment to profitability. In the next section we turn attention to how engagement impacts the individual, including wellbeing, health, and stress reduction.

INDIVIDUAL IMPACT

With all of the added organizationally focused benefits of engagement, we might assume that being engaged is an exhausting experience for employees. Engaged employees are faster and more satisfied, committed, involved, creative, helpful, focused, and profitable. They seem busy, and being that productive has to be strenuous, right? Yet, emerging evidence is equally strong that employees who work in places where they can experience higher levels of engagement also experience individual-level benefits that have the potential to influence their overall quality of life.

For example, employees who report higher levels of engagement also report experiencing lower levels of stress and burnout (Maslach *et al.*, 2001; Schaufeli *et al.*, 2008) and higher levels of accomplishment in their work (Shuck *et al.*, 2013a). While the research on individual outcomes is highly clustered around constructs like wellbeing and stress, research also points to literature that has suggested engaged employees also participate in higher levels of citizenship behaviors (Rich *et al.*, 2010), creating a more positive experience for their co-workers. Employees who are highly engaged report experiencing work more positively than their colleagues who might not be so engaged (Shuck and Reio, 2014).

The benefits of higher levels of employee engagement have been found to extend beyond the boundaries of work. For example, employees who are engaged report lower levels of depression, loneliness, and ostracism as well as lower levels of stress and depersonalizing behaviors (Maslach *et al.*, 2001; Shuck *et al.*, 2011a; Wollard and Shuck, 2011). Engaged employees report higher levels of overall wellbeing, responding positively to statements such as "I am able to have fun" and "I am able to forgive myself for my failures" (Shuck and Reio, 2014). Research would also indicate that being engaged at work has a positive spillover effect into life outside of work that can be operationalized as a heightened sense of wellbeing (Schaufeli *et al.*, 2008; Bakker *et al.*, 2008; Bakker and Schaufeli, 2008; Schaufeli *et al.*, 2011) including better sleep and healthier eating habits (Shuck *et al.*, 2017b). Extending the work by Bailey *et al.* (2017), Shuck *et al.* (2017b) found a moderate relationship between engagement and stress/burnout ($r = -0.32$), engagement and general health ($r = 0.28$) as well as life satisfaction ($r = 0.22$).

Perhaps some context is needed here. The research on engagement up to this point may seem too good to be true. Engaged employees work harder, are more creative, and outperform their colleagues. More, they experience life with less stress, report higher levels of wellbeing, are less frequently burned out, and have higher life satisfaction scores than employees who report lower levels of engagement. Who would not want that? As Bailey *et al.* (2017) reminded us, almost all of the research on employee engagement is cross sectional in nature and while engagement and a host of positive outcomes share a connection, it is not casual. There is a relationship there, and there is a lot of evidence, but no one is suggesting (at least, not yet) that engagement causes less stress, more creativity, and profitability.

At the same time, it is difficult to ignore the mounting evidence that when engagement is present, there are a host of benefits for both the organization and the individual. When engagement is present, additional benefits at the individual level tend to follow on.

In mid-2019, the World Health Organization (WHO) recognized burnout as an official medical diagnosis, and as a result, interest in the connection between burnout and engagement is likely to grow. One of the most cited studies looking at the connection between burnout and engagement is the seminal work by Schaufeli *et al.* (2002), which was one of the first to examine a relationship between the two constructs. The primary purpose of their original work was to examine the factor structure of the UWES, which was at the time of their writing a new measure of engagement. Results confirmed that engagement and burnout were related ($r = -.46$ [sample 1] and $r = -.61$ [sample 2]). Equally standard is the continued work by Schaufeli and Bakker (2004) in looking at the relationship between burnout, engagement, and health outcomes. Results from their work suggested that burnout was more predictive of health outcomes ($R^2 = .37 - .42$) than engagement, which was more predictive of intention to turnover ($R^2 = .9 - .24$). In sum, a host of scholars have looked at the linkage between burnout and engagement, and all have suggested that engagement and burnout share a negative relationship.

As mentioned in Chapters 2 and 4, burnout and engagement have shared a contentious history and very few scholars have explored engagement beyond the UWES-burnout linkage. This has been problematic in the literature due to the potential for construct redundancy (c.f., Cole *et al.*, 2012). One of the only studies to look at the burnout and engagement connection outside of the predominate UWES framework was Shuck *et al.* (2013a), who used the Job Engagement Scale alongside the Iverson *et al.* (1998) exhaustion measure as a means to differentiate the two ideas. Results suggested that engagement and burnout were negatively related ($r = -.44$). Interested readers might explore Buys and Rothmann (2010), Vera *et al.* (2010), Sonnentag *et al.* (2008), Schaufeli *et al.* (2008), and Bakker *et al.* (2008) for more information.

Throughout the engagement literature, wellbeing and health-related outcomes seem to go hand in hand. There is not, however, a wide breadth of research focused on engagement and health, like there has been for other individual and organizational outcomes. The breadth of work is rather small and represents a growing opportunity of potential research that scholars might focus toward. There are, however, a handful of studies that have explored the connection between employee engagement and wellbeing and/ or health as a means to examine how, if at all, experiences of engagement at work might share come connection to health-related outcomes.

For example, results from work by Shuck and Reio (2014) suggested that engagement was negatively related to emotional exhaustion ($r = -.30$) and depersonalization, and positively related to personal accomplishment ($r = .48$) and psychological wellbeing ($r = .37$). Several studies have uncovered a positive association between engagement and positive health outcomes (c.f., Freeney and Fellenz, 2013) as well as negative associations between engagement and poor health outcomes (c.f., Hallberg and Schaufeli, 2006). In one of the most rigorous studies exploring this relationship, Shimazu *et al*. (2012) set out to examine the relationship between engagement, well-being, performance, and workaholism. Using a time-lagged study (interval was ~7 months in between data collection), results showed that workaholism (overwork, or an addiction to work) was related to an increase in health complications and a decrease in overall life satisfaction, while higher levels of engagement were related to lower levels of overall health complications and a steep, positive increase in life satisfaction as well as overall performance. Scholars have additionally explored linkages between engagement and the influence of recovery rest after high levels of engagement and proactive behavior (Sonnentag, 2012; Sonnentag *et al*., 2012; Sonnentag *et al*., 2010), overall life satisfaction (Extremera *et al*., 2012), work ability (Airila *et al*., 2012; Mache *et al*., 2013), and increased levels of overall positive affect (Sonnentag *et al*., 2008).

As an interesting caveat, at the individual level, gender – as a demographic differentiator between engagement levels – has been little covered in the literature. Those studies that have looked at distinction are decidedly mixed (Read and Gorman, 2006). For example, Avery *et al*. (2007) reported that women reported higher levels of engagement ($r = .19$) than their male coworkers, yet research by Yildirim (2008) reported that levels of engagement did not reach statistical significance between males and females. Other scholars (Sprang *et al*., 2007; Schaufeli *et al*., 2006) have suggested that females tend to be at a higher risk of developing unhealthy levels of stress due to competing work and home responsibilities and, consequently, more likely to report burnout and decreased levels of engagement.

Connected, and in regards to very specific health outcomes, the research literature has suggested that chronic workplace stressors – such as long hours, job insecurity, and a lack of work–life balance – contribute to factors that lead to premature aging and even early death (Goh *et al*. (2015a). Approximately 5%–8% of annual healthcare costs have been associated with, and may be attributable to, chronic workplace dysfunctionality (Goh *et al*., 2015b) that research has connected to engagement. More specifically, workplace climates that have high levels of employee engagement are very distinct from those described as dysfunctional, toxic, and chronically stressful (Shuck *et al*., 2017b). Indeed, the research has been clear that engagement does not develop in negative climates (Schaufeli *et al.*, 2008; Bakker and Schaufeli, 2008) and that more constructive and optimistic working conditions where the conditions of engagement are present have an opposite, positive effect on health (Bakker *et al.*, 2013; Shuck *et al.*, 2017b).

The literature on individual impact and outcomes of employee engagement are not yet as robust as the organizational impact research, yet exploratory and emerging reports are very promising. There is a developing narrative suggesting that when employees work in places where they experience engagement, they seem to also reap a host of individual benefits, such as being less stressed, happier with their life, and healthier. Again, caution should be exercised in stretching the bounds of any one study beyond its intended limitations; however, as pointed out by Rynes *et al.* (2012), "there is plenty of evidence of the negative effects of contrasting behaviors such as neglect, incivility, derision, bullying, and abuse" (p. 505) and a mounting case for developing the kinds of workplace conditions that engender higher levels of employee engagement.

Concluding thoughts

There is a growing narrative around the impact of employee engagement. Despite the recognized challenges of some of the research in the engagement space – mainly that much of the research on employee engagement is cross sectional in nature, and consequently difficult to draw contributory claims – it seems, based on the available research, that a host of organizationally and individually focused outcomes is present and connected to experiences of engagement. High levels of employee engagement may or may not cause these factors – additional research is needed that is longitudinal and steeped in objective performance data to make casual claims – but it is difficult to deny the association in the face of such voluminous data.

In sum, results of the available research have suggested that leaders who engender the conditions that support the expression of employee engagement (see Chapter 3) are also likely to enjoy more productive employees (Shuck *et al.*, 2013a), higher levels of innovation and creativity (Barrick *et al.*, 2015; O'Boyle *et al.*, 2012), a more satisfied workforce (Černe *et al.*, 2014), and the potential for higher levels of profitability (Alarcon and Edwards, 2011; Rayton and Yalabik, 2014; Yalabik *et al.*, 2013). The evidence-based narrative around the impact of engagement is about as convincing as you can get – volumes and volumes of work detail the positive impact of engagement – even if the best evidence we have is never definitive, or casual. At this time, the research seems clear cut:

employee engagement is an overall win/win scenario for the employee and employer.

This chapter has attempted to summarize the overarching literature on how engagement has been connected to outcomes that matter to leaders, business performance, and individual employees. To be exhaustive in this domain would be unmanageable; every day new research is published that looks at the outcomes of engagement in a new fashion or perspective across the globe. Notwithstanding, within this short-form book, attempts have been made to identify and detail the seminal and emerging areas of research, in hopes that interested readers and leaders who have the potential to influence the future state and conditions of engagement would consult those sources as a primary lens to learn more. This is the research to practice connection that is deeply needed in all forms of research, but in particular, the emerging area of employee engagement.

The next and final chapter offers some concluding thoughts on the future state of employee engagement as well as final reflections on the history and current practice of engagement, including emerging areas of promising research and practice.

Notes

1 A correlation is a mutual relationship or connection between two or more things. In the case of this book, a correlation represents the strength of relationship between two variables, such as employee engagement and intention to turnover. The closer the number is to either +1.00 or −1.00, the stronger the relationship between the two variables.
2 An effect size is a measure of the magnitude of the phenomenon between two variables. The larger the effect size, the more magnitude of difference between the variables. The larger the effect size, the stronger the effect. The suggested range of effect sizes are: small (.20), medium (.50), and large (.80).

6 Final reflections on employee engagement

Throughout this book, we have covered the breadth of research and scholarship on employee engagement. From tracing historical roots and theoretical frames of reference to exploring measurement applications, as well as overviewing the impact of engagement on both organizational and individual outcomes. Up through this point, however, everything covered in this book has been anchored in the past. The history of employee engagement has already been written. Notwithstanding, the future of employee engagement is remarkably and unapologetically less detailed and remains wide open for innovative application and forward movement.

As detailed early in the first chapter of this book, the momentum of interest of employee engagement shows no signs of slowing. The ideas behind employee engagement are mainstream and, now more than ever, a part of most organizations' corporate strategy. More engagement seems to be the mantra, yet to move forward from stagnant numbers and percentages the concept must move forward in both development and application. From objectification to authentication. Transaction to transformation. And in many ways, theory to practice.

In what follows are brief overviews of emerging areas of growth regarding the future state of employee engagement grounded in the research literature as well as some final reflections on the current and hopefully future state of a concept that has the potential to be massively and positively disruptive. In the next section, broad categories of ideas are cast, followed by a short section on the reality of disengagement, and finally, some closing personal reflections on engaging with the practice of engagement.

Emerging areas of growth in employee engagement

One of the more intriguing ideas emerging in the literature is the shift from an organizational perspective of employee engagement to a more focused, personal, and individual perspective. This has emerged in practice by way of measurement, conceptualization, and trans-disciplinary application across academic areas. Some of this work is so emerging that very little research has been conducted, and the sophistication of tools is still being refined, yet, these areas represent what is to come as scholars and practitioners look to harness the power of a fully engaged workforce.

Within-person variation, daily fluctuation, and experience

Researchers are starting to explore within-person variation of employee engagement and what that means for practice. This is about looking at the individual, day-to-day experiences of human beings and how they are expressing engagement. As more refined measures are developed, the assumptions about how engagement is actually expressed – and experienced – on a daily, moment-to-moment basis are shifting. Instead of collecting data about a single point in time, akin to taking a snapshot of a moment and generalizing that picture to the whole of reality, scholars are now tracking daily – and in some cases, even hourly – fluctuations in engagement.

For example, Breevaart *et al.* (2014) examined the daily influence of transformational leadership, contingent reward, and active management-by-exception (MBE) on followers' daily engagement levels across a defined period of time. Breevaart *et al.* (2014) tracked within-person variation at multiple times throughout a given day over a 34-day period. Their findings suggested that transformational leadership contributed to more favorable work environments, highlighting the importance of leadership in daily experiences of work engagement – and underscoring the power of exploring within-person variations of employee engagement. Tims *et al.* (2011) identified similar findings, again highlighting the important role of a leader in individual daily experiences of engagement, across time and participants. Both studies used a diary study methodology.

To explore within-person variation, scholars have adopted a methodology known as the *diary study methodology*. Much of the research utilizing this methodology originated from the Netherlands and Norway with scholars such as Petrou *et al.* (2012), Xanthopoulou *et al.* (2009), and Ouweneel *et al.* (2012). While rigorous and demanding from both a participant and researcher perspective, these methods are quasi-mixed method in approach, often pairing survey responses alongside frequent entries of narrative into personal journal diaries in response to a series of prompted questions. In this methodology, participants are asked to fill in short-answer questions or respond to quick survey items at multiple points in time for a set level of consecutive time (i.e., ten days, one week, etc.). This methodology allows researchers to examine feelings, behaviors, and judgements in the moment, during natural and normal working conditions, which may not be possible with the cross-sectional type designs which have dominated the engagement landscape. Where traditional surveys assume a level of steadiness over time, diary studies assume that fluctuation is normal, and questions are focused on variations in environment, context, and conditions to explain the natural ebb and flow of employee engagement. For example, a group of participants may be asked to fill out a short survey at the end of the workday for 30 days, or using the experience sampling method, participants react to a small set of questions on their smart devices at interval times throughout a 24-hour period for five days (Bolger *et al.*, 2003). For more information on the diary study methodology, see Bolger *et al.* (2003), Fletcher *et al.* (2017), Kuntsche and Labhart (2013), and Bakker (2014) for details.

In one of the more definitive and explanative articles to date, Xanthopoulou *et al.* (2012) detailed the differences between within-person and between-person variance using employee wellbeing. Here, Xanthopoulou *et al.* (2012) challenged the prevailing assumption that engagement was a static experience, and positioned engagement as dynamic and momentary, connecting to the prevailing perspective of employee engagement detailed throughout this book. Xanthopoulou *et al.* (2012) noted that investigating within person fluctuation helped to refine models of actual moments of engagement, as they were lived, through sophisticated statistical techniques such as multi-level modeling. This allowed researchers to examine why employees who are generally happy most days, may not always be equally happy every day, and more, what impact this could have on their work and working experience. Exploring between-person studies (i.e., traditionally focused research examining how individuals are different either through cross-sectional or longitudinal methods focused on individual differences between Participant A and Participant B) allowed scholars and practitioners to understand more about *The Happy Productive Worker Theory* (Cropanzano and Wright, 2001). The Happy Productive Worker Theory suggests that happy workers are also more productive workers – an interesting and elegantly simplistic idea, yet, it leaves very little room for happy people to have a bad day.

To explore this theory, Bakker (2014) leaned on the Job Demands-Resources Theory in examining daily fluctuations in engagement, offering that fluctuations in work engagement are often a function of the changes in daily job and personal resources. When employees had sufficient resources to meet demands, not surprisingly they were more likely to experience – and report – higher levels of engagement. "Particularly on the days that employees have access to many resources, they are able to cope well with their daily job demands (e.g., work pressure, negative events), and likely interpret these demands as challenges" (p. 1). Employees who experienced more demands than resources were likely to become frustrated and withdrawn.

That is, when demands outweighed resources, meaning was re-evaluated, and disengagement had the potential to set in as a frustrating experience. *Frustration* – or a lack of control over obstacles toward meaningful goals – is a perception variable that has components of an attitude and is just emerging as an area of focus in work and employee engagement.

At present, little work has explored experiences of frustration throughout the human resource or management domains as a focal point. In parallel, however, more recently, researchers have looked at many promising investigations around the impacts of frustration and performance, including frustration and persistence in gaming (Huang *et al.*, 2017), understanding the role between frustration at work and engagement (Ugwu and Onyishi, 2018), and frustration and self-confidence (Fang *et al.*, 2018). This has connections to the emerging ideas of overcapacity and overwork, burnout, and the cumulative effect on outcomes such as health and wellbeing.

The diary study methodology has been modified and adopted for use in the for-profit practice as well, beyond academic research. Pulse surveys, which essentially use the same framework as the experience-sampling methodology, are becoming quite common as an industry standard. Consulting practices are using pulse-type methodologies as a way to connect more meaningfully and frequently with employees to gauge real-time data, in a natural, lived context. Very few for-profit consulting groups are, however, using multi-level modeling techniques to explore within-person variation, but the trend for more frequent, in the moment data is catching on. Perhaps this methodology has been an attempt to more meaningfully capture authentic expressions of employee voice and silence, the next emerging area of research.

Authentic engagement, employee voice, silence

As an artifact of the shift engagement is experiencing from transactional to transformational – from objectification to authentic expression – research on employee voice and silence is taking center stage. Employee voice has been defined as the ubiquitous and discretionary sharing of information in organizations (Liang *et al.*, 2012). This is an emerging and exciting area of research, yet not all scholars agree on how it operates in practice.

Because leadership has been shown to be such an impactful influence on employee engagement, several scholars have examined employee voice from the context of leadership, including transformational leadership (Svendsen and Joensson, 2016; Svendsen *et al.*, 2016), leader trust (Gao *et al.*, 2011), and ethical leadership (Chen and Hou, 2016; Zhu *et al.*, 2015; Elçi *et al.*, 2012). More, several researchers have looked at experiences like supervisor openness to ideas and an employee's willingness to use their voice in their work. Reliably, the research indicates that when a leader shows an openness to new ideas and listening, employees are likely to speak up – and when the open-door policy is not so open, employees tend to stay silent (Tangirala and Ramanujam, 2012). Others have focused exclusively on the linkage between employee engagement and voice (Purcell, 2014; Purcell, 2013; Purcell and Georgiadis, 2007; Robinson, 2018).

While there is some disagreement on whether voice is an antecedent to, or the outcome of job attitudes like employee engagement (Chamberlin *et al.*, 2017), there is a reliable understanding that employee voice is an indicator of authentic expressions of engagement. That is, when employees are engaged, they tend to be more likely to use their voice – and when they are disengaged, they tend to use silence. Pinder and Harlos (2001) defined silence as "the withholding of any form of genuine expression about the individual's behavioral, cognitive and/or affective evaluations of his or her organizational circumstances to persons who are perceived to be capable of effecting change or redress" (p. 334).

Voice has been positioned as a proxy for authentic expressive levels of employee engagement, and more specific to our context, Kahn and Heaphy (2014) positioned employee voice as the often overlooked, relational context of engagement indicative of voice. When employees believe that they matter, and that using their voice will have impact, they engage. Only a handful of studies have, however, explicitly looked at the linkages between employee engagement and voice. Positioned as an outcome, Rees *et al.* (2013) found employee voice to be a predictor of engagement and that trust in senior management and the employer-line manager relationship partially mediated this relationship. Knoll and Redman (2016) identified that the more affectively attached and engaged an employee was to their organization, the more likely they were to exercise their voice. Cumberland *et al.* (2018) highlighted the role of middle management in encouraging employees to use voice as an expression of their engagement. These findings suggested that supervisor openness is positively associated with job satisfaction and employee engagement, but that only engagement was a facilitating variable that stimulated employee voice. In this work, engagement was an antecedent to voice.

Research by Kwon *et al.* (2016) has suggested best practices and propositions to the study of voice and engagement. Using the Job Demands-Resource Model, Kwon *et al.* looked at voice and engagement on three unique levels: macro-level national culture (*the degree of power distance*), meso-level organizational climate (*the extent of empowering leadership and participation*), and micro-level relationship quality between employee and supervisor (*leader–member exchange*). Their framework provided an actionable, strategic, evidence-based approach to voice from an organizational development outlook. In more defined practice, Purcell (2014) suggested that for authentic levels of engagement to be achieved, there must be effective communication systems in place on multiple levels (i.e., both the shop-floor and the board room), consultative committees designed to elicit feedback, and workgroups with employees and their voices at the heart of improving engagement across the organization.

See Kwon *et al.* (2016), Robinson (2018), Cumberland *et al.* (2018), Purcell (2014), and Kahn and Heaphy (2014) for additional details on employee voice and engagement.

The reality of disengagement

In 2011, Wollard offered one of the earliest perspectives on employee disengagement. In her work, she overviewed early statistics on engagement – which indicated less than 30% of employees went to work every day fully engaged – and asked, "So what of the other 70%?" (Wollard, 2011, p. 527). This is a particularly pertinent question and perhaps an opportunity for employee engagement moving forward.

Disengagement has been plagued with a poorly defined theoretical framework and conceptualized haphazardly throughout the research literature. Wollard, as one of the first and seminal scholars to explicitly explore disengagement, defined the construct as being "characterized by the disconnection of individuals from their work roles to protect themselves physically, mentally and/or emotionally from real or perceived threats" (p. 528). Kahn (1990) defined disengagement in terms of withdrawal and defense of preferred self, while Demerouti *et al.* (2001) positioned disengagement as a component of burnout, offering that disengagement could be defined as "distancing oneself from one's work, and experiencing negative attitudes toward the work object, work content, or one's work in general" (Demerouti *et al.*, 2001, p. 501).

While disengagement may not be well conceptualized yet, what seems clear is that disengaged employees push away and distance themselves from their work, intentionally – and there are potentially a lot of disengaged employees. The research on disengagement uses some of the same frameworks covered throughout earlier chapters in this book to explain how the experience happens, including Kahn's (1990) early psychological and contextual work, the burnout perspective, and the Conservations of Resources Theory (COR) – but in the reverse. For example, within the transcripts used in Kahn's (1990) original work, participants reliably cited a lack of meaning, safety, and the availability of resources and their conscious decision to disengage. When employees assessed the situation as unfavorable, they detached and withdrew, and parallel to work by Rich *et al.* (2010) and Shuck *et al.* (2017c), employees protected themselves cognitively, emotionally, and behaviorally (Kahn, 1990). Interested readers might explore work by Rastogi *et al.* (2018), who provided a comprehensive review of the disengagement literature and detailed historical frames of reference.

The impact of disengagement is not fully known, but results have the potential to be distressing. Company revenues in organizations with high levels of engagement are 40% higher than those with low levels of engagement, and revenue is higher in organizations with employees who report higher levels of engagement across the board. Turnover, one of the physical manifestations of disengagement, can range from 30% to 200% of the lost employee's salary (Herman *et al.*, 2003). Fraud, theft, and property loss cost organizations on average 5% of revenues, or US$2.9 trillion, with the average fraud costing an organization US$160,000 (Richards *et al.*, 2010) – an incredibly high number per incident. More, work by Rose *et al.* (2015) and Kulas *et al.* (2007) on dysfunctional leaders and deviant employees detailed that counterproductive work behaviors such as property deviance (theft of merchandise or supplies, unauthorized discounts, falsifying records, etc.) and production deviance (time theft, absenteeism, taking long breaks, leaving early, work withdrawal behaviors) have been linked to hundreds of billions of dollars in losses. As Wollard (2011) offered, coupled with bad economic times, "companies suffer further from substandard work from employees who would like to leave" but do not (p. 528). Research has also been linked to depression, burnout, and significant health outcomes that can have deleterious and long-lasting impacts on physical health.

This book has intentionally focused on employee engagement and the potential positive upside of engaging employees authentically. The transformational power of engagement has been documented, yet the reality of disengagement is for so many people who work, a real and lived experience. The causes, antecedents, and outcomes of disengagement are presently poorly defined, and so this gap in the research represents an incredible opportunity for scholars to explore disengagement in more quality over the next decade. We have much to learn about disengagement and how, using the work detailed throughout this book, we can improve the working experiences of so many who go to work every day. Using what we know about how engagement develops and emerging technologies in the area of measurement, we have the potential to shift work from a transactional perspective to one of more abundance, fulfillment, and meaning that can drive a host of positive, productive, and life-giving outcomes.

Final reflections on employee engagement

This short-form book has been a journey, and so has the history and development of employee engagement. As the topic of employee engagement has matured, it has been refined and grown in sophistication. The research around employee engagement has taken form with grounded frameworks, measurement options, and definitions. As this short-form book comes to a close, perhaps a few brief anecdotal observations are warranted.

As we have detailed the development of employee engagement and what it means for our work, I should be clear that in my opinion, engagement is not performance. Employee engagement is not about being faster, better, and stronger, although the literature is clear (over and over and over again) that engaged employees might display those qualities. Indeed, engaged employees may very well be faster and more productive, which is why so many leaders desire an engaged workforce – and will do almost anything to reach that goal. At its very core, employee engagement is a formidable, authentically individual state of motivation. Engagement is also not a strategy. Employee engagement is an outcome of a strategy but is not a strategy in and of itself. Employee engagement is not a pulse survey, a top ten list of activities, or interview data. Employee engagement is not program, a new process, or a strategic plan although programs, processes, and plans can all improve engagement when the employee experience is placed at the center of that plan.

Employee engagement – as I have detailed and grounded throughout this book – is about the individual. And a belief that work and contributions matter. Employee engagement happens when an employee believes that if they give of their engagement, their organization (often viewed through the lens of who they believe to be their immediate supervisor) will support them and have their interests in mind as equally as they have their own.

Employee engagement cannot be demanded; it can only be offered. It cannot be mandated through policies and procedures. Great organizations are made from teams who are willing to be great, and great teams are made from individuals who will risk being engaged. Employee engagement is not about expectation as much as it is about invitation. That invitation is about feeling included – not an empty promise. Engagement that is demanded is compliance, and while compliance and engagement have seemingly similar outcomes on the surface, one is transactional while the other is transformational. Employee engagement is not flat like other more unidimensional variables; it is just as dynamic and changing as the person being asked to be more fully engaged.

As we close, a note about practice. The core purpose of this book has been to overview the wide and deep history of employee engagement research: definitions, frameworks, and seminal scholars in the field. The practice of engagement has been embedded within each chapter. Unfortunately, this book does not offer a Top 10 List for improving employee engagement. That would be insensitive and outside the scope of my intended purpose.

But like a red thread woven throughout each chapter, there are pieces of the puzzle throughout the range of scholarship on engagement that should explicitly inform practice. For example, practitioners interested in improving employee engagement might focus on implementing recognition strategies that support core experiences, training leaders to show up differently and approaching their work from a place of dignity and presence, elevating learning and development strategies for all levels of employees, pointing employees to their future through career mapping and pathing, developing systems that support psychological safety, making time to listen and talk with employees throughout the organization, empowering voice and acknowledging the role of silence through groups and defined channels, focusing on fair and equitable benefits and human resource systems that are dignified and procedurally and distributively fair, preparing leaders and managers to have empowering and future-focused one-on-one conversations, and finally, finding authentic ways to communicate every day how important, meaningful, and valued each employee is to their work. The context from organization to organization will be different – and should be – and thus, practices will look different, but the core principles – which have been exhaustively and extensively detailed throughout the research literature – remain steady. Indeed, the future and viability of employee engagement will lie in the ability for social science researchers to continue asking the question: does engagement matter, and if it does, how can we help our employee's express it?

More, identifying opportunities for refined, intentional, longitudinal intervention work will be the way that employee engagement can and will influence the emerging landscape of organizations over the next millennia as well as how work and the working context can be shaped. To move in that direction, we will need evidence-based intervention studies that qualify the research around engagement and point practitioners toward improved practice in ways they can both trust and implement. Contextual sensitivity of the research and practice will need to merge as engagement grows in both theory and practice.

But we should never lose sight. When all is said and done, employee engagement is about the individual. The human being who goes to work every day. The thirst for meaning and value in that work, and the outcomes connected to those psychological experiences. As we move forward, continuing to document the human condition of work will be essential for developing the future state of employee engagement.

References

Airila, A., Hakanen, J., Punakallio, A., Lusa, S., and Luukkonen, R. 2012. Is work engagement related to work ability beyond working conditions and lifestyle factors? *International Archives of Occupational Environmental Health*, 85, 915–925.

Alarcon, G. M., and Edwards, J. M. 2011. The relationship of engagement, job satisfaction and turnover intentions. *Stress and Health*, 27, e294–e298.

Albrecht, S. L. 2010. *Handbook of employee engagement: Perspectives, issues, research and practice.* Cheltenham, UK: Edward Elgar Publishing.

Arakawa, D., and Greenberg, M. 2007. Optimistic managers and their influence on productivity and employee engagement in a technology organisation: Implications for coaching psychologists. *International Coaching Psychology Review*, 2, 78–89.

Ashforth, B. E., and Mael, F. A. 1989. Social identity theory and the organization. *The Academy of Management Review*, 14, 20–39.

Avery, D. R., Mckay, P. F., and Wilson, D. C. 2007. Engaging the aging workforce: The relationship between perceived age similarity, satisfaction with coworkers, and employee engagement. *Journal of Applied Psychology*, 92, 1542–1556.

Bailey, C., Madden, A., Alfes, K., and Fletcher, L. 2017. The meaning, antecedents and outcomes of employee engagement: A narrative synthesis. *International Journal of Management Reviews*, 19, 31–53.

Bailey, C., Madden, A., Alfes, K., Fletcher, L., Robinson, D., Holmes, J., Buzzeo, J., and Currie, G. 2015. Evaluating the evidence on employee engagement and its potential benefits to NHS staff: A narrative synthesis of the literature. *Health Services Delivery Research*, 3, 1–424.

Bakker, A. B. 2014. Daily fluctuations in work engagement. *European Psychologist*, 19(4), 227–236.

Bakker, A. B., and Schaufeli, W. B. 2008. Positive organizational behavior: Engaged employees in flourishing organizations. *Journal of Organizational Behavior*, 29, 147–154.

Bakker, A. B., Schaufeli, W. B., Leiter, M. P., and Taris, T. W. 2008. Work engagement: An emerging concept in occupational health psychology. *Work & Stress*, 22, 187–200.

Bakker, A. B., Shimazu, A., Demerouti, E., Shimada, K., and Kawakami, N. 2013. Work engagement versus workaholism: A test of the spillover-crossover model. *Journal of Managerial Psychology*, 29, 63–80.

Barrett, L. F., and Russell, J. A. 1999. The structure of current affect: Controversies and emerging consensus. *Current Directions in Psychological Science*, 8, 10–14.

Barrick, M. R., Mount, M. K., and Li, N. 2013. The theory of purposeful work behavior: The role of personality, higher-order goals, and job characteristics. *Academy of Management Review*, 38, 132–153.

Barrick, M. R., Thurgood, G. R., Smith, T. A., and Courtright, S. H. 2015. Collective organizational engagement: Linking motivational antecedents, strategic implementation, and firm performance. *Academy of Management Journal*, 58, 111–135.

Baumruk, R. 2004. The missing link: The role of employee engagement in business success. *Workspan*, *47*(11), 48–52.

Biggs, A., Brough, P., and Barbour, J. P. 2014. Strategic alignment with organizational priorities and work engagement: A multi-wave analysis. *Journal of Organizational Behavior*, 35, 301–317.

Binneweis, C., and Fetzer, B. 2010. Affective states and affect regulation as antecedents of dynamic work engagement. *In:* Albrecht, S. L. (ed.) *The handbook of employee engagement: Perspectives, issues, research and practice.* Cheltenham, UK: Edward Elgar Publishing Limited.

Bledow, R., Schmitt, A., Frese, M., and Kühnel, J. 2011. The affective shift model of work engagement. *Journal of Applied Psychology*, 96, 1246.

Bolger, N., Davis, A., and Rafaeli, E. 2003. Diary methods: Capturing life as it is lived. *Annual Review of Psychology*, 54, 579–616.

Breevaart, K., Bakker, A., Hetland, J., Demerouti, E., Olsen, O. K., and Espevik, R. 2014. Daily transactional and transformational leadership and daily employee engagement. *Journal of Occupational and Organizational Psychology*, 87, 138–157.

Brief, A. P., and Weiss, H. M. 2002. Organizational behavior: Affect in the workplace. *Annual Review of Psychology*, 53, 279–307.

Briner, R. B. 2014. What is employee engagement and does it matter? An evidence-based approach. *The Future of Engagement Thought Piece Collection*, 51.

Briner, R. B. 2015. What's the evidence for . . . evidence-based HR? *HR Magazine*.

Brown, A. D., and Starkey, K. 2000. Organizational identity and learning: A psychodynamic perspective. *Academy of Management Review*, 25, 102–120.

Brown, S. P. 1996. A meta-analysis and review of organizational research on job involvement. *Psychological Bulletin*, 120, 235–255.

Brown, S. P., and Leigh, T. W. 1996. A new look at psychological climate and its relationship to job involvement, effort, and performance. *Journal of Applied Psychology*, 81, 358–368.

Buckingham, M., and Coffman, C. 1999. *First, break all the rules: What the world's greatest managers do differently.* New York, NY: Simon and Schuster.

Buys, C., and Rothmann, S. 2010. Burnout and engagement of reformed church ministers. *South African Journal of Industrial Psychology*, 36, 1–11.

Carasco-Saul, M., Kim, W., and Kim, T. 2015. Leadership and employee engagement: Proposing research agendas through a review of literature. *Human Resource Development Review*, 14, 38–63.

Černe, M., Nerstad, C. G. L., Dysvik, A., and Škerlavaj, M. 2014. What goes around comes around: Knowledge hiding, perceived motivational climate, and creativity. *Academy of Management Journal*, 57, 172–192.

Chamberlin, M., Newton, D. W., and Lepine, J. A. 2017. A meta-analysis of voice and its promotive and prohibitive forms: Identification of key associations, distinctions, and future research directions. *Personnel Psychology*, 70, 11–71.

Chen, A. S.-Y., and Hou, Y.-H. 2016. The effects of ethical leadership, voice behavior and climates for innovation on creativity: A moderated mediation examination. *The Leadership Quarterly*, 27, 1–13.

Christian, M. S., Garza, A. S., and Slaughter, J. E. 2011. Work engagement: A quantitative review and test of its relations with task and contextual performance. *Personnel Psychology*, 64, 89–136.

Cole, M. S., Walter, F., Bedeian, A. G., and O'boyle, E. H. 2012. Job burnout and employee engagement: A meta-analytic examination of construct proliferation. *Journal of Management*, 38, 1550–1581.

Cooper Thomas, H., Leighton, N., Xu, J., and Knight-Turvey, N. 2010. Measuring change: Does engagement flourish, fade, or stay true. *In:* Albrecht, S. L. (ed.) *Handbook of employee engagement.* Auckland, New Zealand: Edward Elgar Publishing.

Crawford, E. R., Lepine, J. A., and Rich, B. L. 2010. Linking job demands and resources to employee engagement and burnout: A theoretical extension and meta-analytic test. *Journal of Applied Psychology*, 95, 834.

Cropanzano, R., and Wright, T. A. 2001. When a "happy" worker is really a "productive" worker: A review and further refinement of the happy-productive worker thesis. *Consulting Psychology Journal: Practice and Research*, 53, 182.

Cumberland, D. M., Shuck, B., Immekus, J., and Alagaraja, M. 2018. An emergent understanding of influences on managers' voices in SMEs. *Leadership & Organization Development Journal*, 39, 234–247.

Czarnowsky, M. 2008. *Learning's role in employee engagement: An ASTD research study.* Alexandria, VA: American Society for Training Development.

Dalal, R. S., Baysinger, M., Brummel, B. J., and Lebreton, J. M. 2012. The relative importance of employee engagement, other job attitudes, and trait affect as predictors of job performance. *Journal of Applied Social Psychology*, 42, E295–E325.

Demerouti, E., Bakker, A. B., Nachreiner, F., and Schaufeli, W. B. 2001. The job demands-resources model of burnout. *Journal of Applied psychology*, 86, 499.

De Villiers, J. R., and Stander, M. W. 2011. Psychological empowerment, work engagement and turnover intention: The role of leader relations and role clarity in a financial institution. *Journal of Psychology in Africa*, 21, 405–412.

Diedericks, E., and Rothmann, S. 2013. Flourishing of infomraiton technology professionals: The role of work engagement and satisfaction. *Journal of Psychology in Arfica*, 23, 225–233.

Eagly, A. H., and Chaiken, S. 1993. *The psychology of attitudes.* San Diego, CA: Harcourt Brace Jovanovich College Publishers.

Elçi, M., Şener, I., Aksoy, S., and Alpkan, L. 2012. The impact of ethical leadership and leadership effectiveness on employees' turnover intention: The mediating role of work related stress. *Procedia-Social and Behavioral Sciences*, 58, 289–297.

Extremera, N., Sánchez-García, M., Durán, M. A., and Rey, L. 2012. Examining the psychometric properties of the utrecht work engagement scale in two Spanish multi-occupational samples. *International Journal of Selection Assessment*, 20, 105–110.

Fairlie, P. 2011. Meaningful work, employee engagement, and other key employee outcomes: Implications for human resource development. *Advances in Developing Human Resources*, 13, 508–525.

Fang, H., He, B., Fu, H., Zhang, H., Mo, Z., and Meng, L. 2018. A surprising source of self-motivation: Prior competence frustration strengthens one's motivation to win in another competence-supportive activity. *Frontiers in Human Neuroscience*, 12.

Fleming, J. H., and Asplund, J. 2007. *Human sigma: Managing the employee-customer encounter*. New York: Simon and Schuster.

Fletcher, L. 2016a. How can personal development lead to increased engagement? The roles of meaningfulness and perceived line manager relations. *The International Journal of Human Resource Management*, 1–24.

Fletcher, L. 2016b. Training perceptions, engagement, and performance: Comparing work engagement and personal role engagement. *Human Resource Development International*, 19, 4–26.

Fletcher, L. 2017. The everyday experiences of personal role engagement: What matters most? *Human Resource Development Quarterly*, 28, 451–479.

Fletcher, L., Bailey, C., and Gilman, M. W. 2017. Fluctuating levels of personal role engagement within the working day: A multilevel study. *Human Resource Management Journal*, 28, 128–147.

Frank, F. D., Finnegan, R. P., and Taylor, C. R. 2004. The race for talent: Retaining and engaging workers in the 21st century. *Human Resource Planning*.

Freeney, Y., and Fellenz, M. R. 2013. Work engagement as a key driver of quality of care: A study with midwives. *Journal of Health Organization Management Science*, 27, 330–349.

Freud, S. 1922. *Group psychology* and *the analysis of the* ego. London: International Psychoanalytic Press.

Fugate, M., Harrison, S., and Kinicki, A. J. 2011. Thoughts and feelings about organizational change: A field test of appraisal theory. *Journal of Leadership & Organizational Studies*, 18, 421–437.

Gao, L., Janssen, O., and Shi, K. 2011. Leader trust and employee voice: The moderating role of empowering leader behaviors. *The Leadership Quarterly*, 22, 787–798.

Garg, K., Dar, I. A., and Mishra, M. 2018. Job satisfaction and work engagement: A study using private sector bank managers. *Advances in Developing Human Resources*, 20, 58–71.

Goffman, E. 1961. *The presentation of self in everyday life*. London: Anchor Books.

Goh, J., Pfeffer, J., and Zenios, S. A. 2015a. Exposure to harmful workplace practices could account for inequality in life spans across different demographic groups. *Health Affairs*, 34, 1761–1768.

Goh, J., Pfeffer, J., and Zenios, S. A. 2015b. The relationship between workplace stressors and mortality and health costs in the United States. *Management Science*.

Grant, A. M. 2008. Employees without a cause: The motivational effects of prosocial impact in public service. *International Public Management Journal*, 11, 48–66.

Griffin, M. A., Parker, S. K., and Neal, A. 2008. Is behavioral engagement a distinct and useful construct? *Industrial and Organizational Psychology*, 1, 48–51.

Gruman, J. A., and Saks, A. M. 2011. Performance management and employee engagement. *Human Resource Management Review*, 21, 123–136.

Guest, D. 2014. Employee engagement: A sceptical analysis. *Journal of Organizational Effectiveness: People and Performance*, 1, 141–156.

Hackman, J. R., and Oldham, G. R. 1980. *Work redesign*. Reading, MA: Addison-Wesley.

Hallberg, U. E., and Schaufeli, W. B. 2006. "Same same" but different? Can work engagement be discriminated from job involvement and organizational commitment? *European Psychologist*, 11, 119.

Harrison, D. A., Newman, D. A., and Roth, P. L. 2006. How important are job attitudes? Meta-analytic comparisons of integrative behavioral outcomes and time sequences. *Academy of Management Journal*, 49, 305–325.

Harter, J. K., Schmidt, F. L., Asplund, J. W., Killham, E. A., and Agrawal, S. 2010. Causal impact of employee work perceptions on the bottom line of organizations. *Perspectives on Psychological Science*, 5, 378–389.

Harter, J. K., Schmidt, F. L., and Hayes, T. L. 2002. Business-unit-level relationship between employee satisfaction, employee engagement, and business outcomes: A meta-analysis. *Journal of Applied Psychology*, 87, 268–279.

Harter, J. K., Schmidt, F. L., and Keyes, C. L. 2003. Well-being in the workplace and its relationship to business outcomes: A review of the Gallup studies. *In: Flourishing: Positive psychology the life well-lived*. Lincoln, NE: Gallup.

Herman, R. E., Olivo, T. G., and Gioia, J. L. 2003. Impending crisis. Oakhill Press: Winchester, Virginia.

Hernandez, M., and Guarana, C. L. 2018. An examination of the temporal intricacies of job engagement. *Journal of Management*, 44, 1711–1735.

Hewitt, A. 2015. *Actively disengaged and staying: Dealing with prisoners in the workplace* [Online]. Minneapolis, MN: Modern Survey. Available at: www.modern survey.com/wp-content/uploads/2016/10/Actively-Disengaged-Staying.pdf.

Hirschfeld, R. R., and Thomas, C. H. 2008. Representations of trait engagement: Integration, additions, and mechanisms. *Industrial and Organizational Psychology*, 1, 63–66.

Hochschild, A. R. 1979. Emotion work, feeling rules, and social structure. *The American Journal of Sociology*, 85, 551–575.

Huang, H.-C., Liao, G.-Y., Chiu, K.-L., and Teng, C.-I. 2017. How is frustration related to online gamer loyalty? A synthesis of multiple theories. *Cyberpsychology, Behavior, and Social Networking*, 20, 683–688.

Hulin, C. L., and Judge, T. A. 2003. Job attitudes. *Handbook of Psychology*, 255–276.

Iverson, R. D., Olekalns, M., and Erwin, P. 1998. Affectivity, organizational stressors, and absenteeism: A causal model of burnout and its consequences. *Journal of Vocational Behavior*, 52, 1–23.

Jackson, C. L., Colquitt, J. A., Wesson, M. J., and Zapata-Phelan, C. P. 2006. Psychological collectivism: A measurement validation and linkage to group member performance. *Journal of Applied Psychology*, 91, 884–899.

James, J. B., Mckechnie, S., and Swanberg, J. 2011. Predicting employee engagement in an age-diverse retail workforce. *Journal of Organizational Behavior*, 32, 173–196.

Jones, N. 2012. *Full circle: Employee engagement in the welsh public service*. Bangor, Wales: Bangor University.

Jones, N., Sambrook, S., and Doloriert, C. 2011. Employee engagement in the Welsh public service: An ethnographic approach. *15th International Research Society for Public Management*. Dublin, Ireland: Dublin University.

Joo, B.-K., Zigarmi, D., Nimon, K., and Shuck, B. 2017. Work cognition and psychological well-being: The role of cognitive engagement as a partial mediator. *The Journal of Applied Behavioral Science*, 53, 446–469.

Judge, T. A., Heller, D., and Mount, M. K. 2002. Five-factor model of personality and job satisfaction: A meta-analysis. *Journal of Applied Psychology*, 87, 530–541.

Kahn, W. A. 1990. Psychological conditions of personal engagement and disengagement at work. *Academy of Management Journal*, 33, 692–724.

Kahn, W. A. 1992. To be fully there: Psychological presence at work. *Human Relations*, 45, 321–349.

Kahn, W. A. 2010. The essence of engagement: Lessons from the field. *In:* Albrecht, S. L. (ed.) *Handbook of employee engagement: Perspectives, issues, research and practice*. Cheltenham, UK: Edward Elgar.

Kahn, W. A., and Heaphy, E. 2014. Relational contexts of personal engagement at work. *In:* Truss, C., Alfes, K., Delbridge, R., Shantz, A., and Soane, E. (eds.) *Employee engagement in theory and practice*. Milton Park, Abingdon, Oxfordshire: Routledge.

Kanungo, R. N. 1982. Measurement of job and work involvement. *Journal of Applied Psychology*, 67, 341.

Keenoy, T. 2013. Engagement: A murmuration of objects? *In:* Truss, C., Delbridge, R., Alfes, K., Shantz, A., and Soane, E. (eds.) *Employee engagement in theory and practice*. New York, NY: Routledge.

Kelleher, B. 2013. *Employee engagement for dummies*. Hoboken, NJ: John Wiley & Sons.

Ketter, P. 2008. What's the big deal about employee engagement? *T+D*, 62(1), 45–49.

Kim, W., Kolb, J. A., and Kim, T. 2013. The relationship between work engagement and performance: A review of empirical literature and a proposed research agenda. *Human Resource Development Review*, 12, 248–276.

Knoll, M., and Redman, T. 2016. Does the presence of voice imply the absence of silence? The necessity to consider employees' affective attachment and job engagement. *Human Resource Management*, 55, 829–844.

Kühnel, J., Sonnentag, S., and Westman, M. 2009. Does work engagement increase after a short respite? The role of job involvement as a double-edged sword. *Journal of Occupational and Organizational Psychology*, 82, 575–594.

Kulas, J. T., Mcinnerney, J. E., Demuth, R. F., and Jadwinski, V. 2007. Employee satisfaction and theft: Testing climate perceptions as a mediator. *The Journal of Psychology*, 141, 389–402.

Kuntsche, E., and Labhart, F. 2013. Using personal cell phones for ecological momentary assessment: An overview of current developments. *European Psychologist*, 18, 3.

Kuppens, P., Tuerlinckx, F., Russell, J. A., and Barrett, L. F. 2013. The relation between valence and arousal in subjective experience. *Psychological Bulletin*, 139, 917–940.

Kwon, B., Farndale, E., and Park, J. G. 2016. Employee voice and work engagement: Macro, meso, and micro-level drivers of convergence? *Human Resource Management Review*, 26, 327–337.

Langelaan, S., Bakker, A. B., Van Doornen, L. J., and Schaufeli, W. B. 2006. Burnout and work engagement: Do individual differences make a difference? *Personality and Individual Differences*, 40, 521–532.

Lauring, J., and Selmer, J. 2015. Job engagement and work outcomes in a cognitively demanding context: The case of expatriate academics. *Personnel Review*, 44, 629–647.

Lawler, E. E., and Hall, D. T. 1970. Relationship of job characteristics to job involvement, satisfaction, and intrinsic motivation. *Journal of Applied Psychology*, 54, 305.

Lazarus, R. S. 1982. Thoughts on the relations between emotion and cognition. *American Psychologist*, 37, 1019.

Lazarus, R. S. 1984. On the primacy of cognition. *American Psychologist*, 39, 124–129.

Leiter, M. P., and Maslach, C. 2017. Burnout and engagement: Contributions to a new vision. *Burnout Research*, 5, 55–57.

Liang, J., Farh, C. I., and Farh, J.-L. 2012. Psychological antecedents of promotive and prohibitive voice: A two-wave examination. *Academy of Management Journal*, 55, 71–92.

Locke, E. A. 1976. The nature and causes of job satisfaction. *Handbook of Industrial and Organizational Psychology*, 1, 1297–1343.

Lockwood, N. R. 2007. Leveraging employee engagement for competitive advantage. *Society for Human Resource Management*, 1, 1–12.

Lodahl, T. M., and Kejnar, M. 1965. The definition and measurement of job involvement. *Journal of Applied Psychology*, 49, 24.

Lok, P., and Crawford, J. 1999. The relationship between commitment and organizational culture, subculture, leadership style and job satisfaction in organizational change and development. *Leadership Organization Development Journal*, 20, 365–374.

Lu, L., Lu, A. C. C., Gursoy, D., and Neale, N. R. 2016. Work engagement, job satisfaction, and turnover intentions: A comparison between supervisors and line-level employees. *International Journal of Contemporary Hospitality Management*, 28, 737–761.

Macey, W. H., and Schneider, B. 2008. The meaning of employee engagement. *Industrial and Organizational Psychology*, 1, 3–30.

Mache, S., Danzer, G., Klapp, B. F., and Groneberg, D. A. 2013. Surgeons' work ability and performance in surgical care: Relations between organisational predictors, work engagement and work ability. *Langenbeck's Archives of Surgery*, 398, 317–325.

Mahon, E. G., Taylor, S. N., and Boyatzis, R. E. 2014. Antecedents of organizational engagement: Exploring vision, mood and perceived organizational support with emotional intelligence as a moderator. *Frontiers in Psychology*, 5, 129–139.

Maslach, C., and Jackson, S. E. 1981. The measurement of experienced burnout. *Journal of Occupational Behaviour*, 2, 99–113.

Maslach, C., Jackson, S. E., and Leiter, M. P. 1996. *Maslach burnout inventory manual*. Palo Alto, CA: Consulting Psychologists Press.

Maslach, C., Jackson, S. E., Leiter, M. P., Schaufeli, W. B., and Schwab, R. L. 1986. *Maslach burnout inventory manual*. 3rd Edition. Menlo Park, CA: Consulting Psychologist's Press.

Maslach, C., Schaufeli, W. B., and Leiter, M. P. 2001. Job burnout. *Annual Review of Psychology*, 52, 397–422.

Maslow, A. H. 1968. *Toward a psychology of being*. New York, NY: Van Nostrand.

Maslow, A. H. 1970. *Motivation and personality*. New York: Longman.

May, D. R., Gilson, R. L., and Harter, L. M. 2004. The psychological conditions of meaningfulness, safety and availability and the engagement of the human spirit at work. *Journal of Occupational and Organizational Psychology*, 77, 11–37.

Merton, R. K., and Merton, R. C. 1968. *Social theory and social structure*. New York: Simon and Schuster.

Meyer, J. P., and Allen, N. J. 1997. *Commitment in the workplace: Theory, research, and application*. Thousand Oaks, CA: Sage.

Meyer, J. P., Stanley, D. J., Herscovitch, L., and Topolnytsky, L. 2002. Affective, continuance, and normative commitment to the organization: A meta-analysis of antecedents, correlates, and consequences. *Journal of Vocational Behavior*, 61, 20–52.

Meyer, R. D., Dalal, R. S., and Hermida, R. 2010. A review and synthesis of situational strength in the organizational sciences. *Journal of Management*, 36, 121–140.

Mowday, R. T., Steers, R. M., and Porter, L. W. 1979. The measurement of organizational commitment. *Journal of Vocational Behavior*, 14, 224–247.

Newman, D. A., and Harrison, D. A. 2008. Been there, bottled that: Are state and behavioral work engagement new and useful construct "wines"? *Industrial Organizational Psychology*, 1, 31–35.

Newman, D. A., Joseph, D. L., and Hulin, C. L. 2010. Job attitudes and employee engagement: Considering the "A-factor". *In:* Albrecht, S. L. (ed.) *Handbook of employee engagement: Perspectives, issues, research, and practice*. Chettenham, UK: Edward Elgar Publishing Limited.

Newman, D. A., Joseph, D. L., Sparkman, T. E., and Carpenter, N. C. 2011. Invited reaction: The work cognition inventory: Initial evidence of construct validity. *Human Resource Development Quarterly*, 22, 37–47.

Nimon, K., Shuck, B., and Zigarmi, D. 2016a. Construct overlap between employee engagement and job satisfaction: A function of semantic equivalence? *Journal of Happiness Studies*, 17, 1149–1171.

Nimon, K., Shuck, B., and Zigarmi, D. 2016b. The tie that binds employee engagement and job attitudes: Harmonious passion and work affect? *In:* Moats, J. (ed.) *Academy of Human Resource Development International Conference of the Americas*. Jacksonville, FL: Proceedings of the Academy of Human Resource Development Conference.

Nimon, K., and Zigarmi, D. 2014. The work cognition inventory: Initial evidence of construct validity for the revised form. *Journal of Career Assessment*, 23, 117–136.

Nimon, K., Zigarmi, D., Houson, D., Witt, D., and Diehl, J. 2011. The work cognition inventory: Initial evidence of construct validity. *Human Resource Development Quarterly*, 22, 7–35.

O'boyle, E. H., Jr., Forsyth, D. R., Banks, G. C., and Mcdaniel, M. A. 2012. A meta-analysis of the Dark Triad and work behavior: A social exchange perspective. *Journal of Applied Psychology*, 97, 557–579.

Oldham, G. R. 2012. The design of jobs: A strategy for enhancing the positive outcomes of individuals at work. *In:* Spreitzer, G. M., and Cameron, K. S. (eds.) *The

Oxford handbook of positive organizational scholarship. New York, NY: Oxford University Press.

Ouweneel, E., Le Blanc, P. M., Schaufeli, W. B., and Van Wijhe, C. I. 2012. Good morning, good day: A diary study on positive emotions, hope, and work engagement. *Human Relations*, 65, 1129–1154.

Owen, J., Rhoades, G., Shuck, B., Fincham, F. D., Stanley, S., Markman, H., and Knopp, K. 2014. Commitment uncertainty: A theoretical overview. *Couple and Family Psychology: Research and Practice*, 3, 207–219.

Owens, B. P., Baker, W. E., Sumpter, D. M., and Cameron, K. S. 2016. Relational energy at work: Implications for job engagement and job performance. *Journal of Applied Psychology*, 101, 35.

Parker, S. K., and Griffin, M. A. 2011. Understanding active psychological states: Embedding engagement in a wider nomological net and closer attention to performance. *European Journal of Work and Organizational Psychology*, 20, 60–67.

Paullay, I. M., Alliger, G. M., and Stone-Romero, E. F. 1994. Construct validation of two instruments designed to measure job involvement and work centrality. *Journal of Applied Psychology*, 79, 224.

Petrou, P., Demerouti, E., Peeters, M. C., Schaufeli, W. B., and Hetland, J. 2012. Crafting a job on a daily basis: Contextual correlates and the link to work engagement. *Journal of Organizational Behavior*, 33, 1120–1141.

Pinder, C. C., and Harlos, K. P. 2001. Employee silence: Quiescence and acquiescence as responses to perceived injustice. *In: Research in personnel and human resources management.* Bingley, UK: Emerald Group Publishing Limited.

Porath, C. L., and Pearson, C. M. 2012. Emotional and behavioral responses to workplace incivility and the impact of hierarchical status. *Journal of Applied Social Psychology*, 42, E326–E357.

Potgieter, L. 2016. *10 steps that ensure employee engagement success* [Online]. Engagement Strategies Medie. Available at: www.enterpriseengagement.org/articles/content/8289281/10-steps-that-ensure-employee-engagement-success/ [Accessed June 20th 2016].

Pugh, S. D., Dietz, J., Brief, A. P., and Wiley, J. W. 2008. Looking inside and out: The impact of employee and community demographic composition on organizational diversity climate. *Journal of Applied Psychology*, 93, 1422–1428.

Purcell, J. 2013. Employee voice and engagement. *In:* Truss, C., Delbridge, R., Alfes, K., Shantz, A., and Soane, E. (eds.) *Employee engagement in theory and practice.* London: Routledge.

Purcell, J. 2014. Disengaging from engagement. *Human Resource Management Journal*, 24, 241–254.

Purcell, J., and Georgiadis, K. 2007. Why should employers bother with worker voice? *In:* Freeman, R., Boxall, P., and Haynes, P. (eds.) *What workers say: Employee voice in the Anglo-American workplace.* Ithaca, NY: Cornell University, ILR Press.

Rastogi, A., Pati, S. P., Krishnan, T. N., & Krishnan, S. (2018). Causes, contingencies, and consequences of disengagement at work: an integrative literature review. *Human Resource Development Review*, *17*(1), 62–94. doi:10.1177/1534484317754160

Rayton, B. A., and Yalabik, Z. Y. 2014. Work engagement, psychological contract breach and job satisfaction. *The International Journal of Human Resource Management*, 25, 2382–2400.

Read, J. N. G., and Gorman, B. K. 2006. Gender inequalities in US adult health: The interplay of race and ethnicity. *Social Science & Medicine*, 62, 1045–1065.

Rees, C., Alfes, K., and Gatenby, M. 2013. Employee voice and engagement: Connections and consequences. *The International Journal of Human Resource Management*, 24, 2780–2798.

Resick, C. J., Baltes, B. B., and Shantz, C. W. 2007. Person-organization fit and work-related attitudes and decisions: Examining interactive effects with job fit and conscientiousness. *Journal of Applied Psychology*, 92, 1446–1455.

Rhoades, L., Eisenberger, R., and Armeli, S. 2001. Affective commitment to the organization: The contribution of perceived organizational support. *Journal of Applied Psychology*, 86, 825–836.

Rich, B. L. 2006. *Job engagement: Construct validation and relationships with job satisfaction, job involvement, and intrinsic motivation.* Gainesville: University of Florida.

Rich, B. L., Lepine, J. A., and Crawford, E. R. 2010. Job engagement: Antecedents and effects on job performance. *Academy of Management Journal*, 53, 617–635.

Richards, D. A., Melancon, B. C., and Ratley, J. D. 2010. *Managing the business risk of fraud: A practical guide.* Institute of Internal Auditors, American Institute of Certified Public Accountants and Association of Certified Fraud Examiners.

Richman, A. 2006. Everyone wants an engaged workforce how can you create it. *Workspan*, *49*(1), 36–39.

Riketta, M., and Landerer, A. 2002. Organizational commitment, accountability, and work behavior: A correlational study. *Social Behavior Personality: An International Journal*, 30, 653–660.

Robinson Jr, J. R. (2018). Employee engagement: Exploring the experiences of how voice and silence relate to public sector employees' feeling of being engaged. PhD Dissertation. ProQuest Dissertation Publishing, George Washington University, USA.

Rose, K., Shuck, B., Twyford, D., and Bergman, M. 2015. Skunked an integrative review exploring the consequences of the dysfunctional leader and implications for those employees who work for them. *Human Resource Development Review*, 14, 64–90.

Rothbard, N. P. 2001. Enriching or depleting? The dynamics of engagement in work and family roles. *Administrative Science Quarterly*, 46, 655–684.

Rurkkhum, S., and Bartlett, K. R. 2012. The relationship between employee engagement and organizational citizenship behaviour in Thailand. *Human Resource Development International*, 15, 157–174.

Russell, J. A., and Barrett, L. F. 1999. Core affect, prototypical emotional episodes, and other things called emotion: Dissecting the elephant. *Journal of Personality Social Psychology*, 76, 805.

Rynes, S., Bartunek, J., Dutton, J., and Margolis, J. 2012. Care and compassion through an organizational lens: Opening up new possibilities. *Academy of Management Review*, 37, 502–523.

Saks, A. M. 2006. Antecedents and consequences of employee engagement. *Journal of Managerial Psychology*, 21, 600–619.

Saks, A. M. 2008. The meaning and bleeding of employee engagement: How muddy is the water? *Industrial and Organizational Psychology*, 1, 40–43.

Saks, A. M. 2019. Antecedents and consequences of employee engagement revisited. *Journal of Organizational Effectiveness: People and Performance*, 21, 600–619.

Saks, A. M., and Gruman, J. A. 2014. What do we really know about employee engagement? *Human Resource Development Quarterly*, 25, 155–182.

Salanova, M., Agut, S., and Peiró, J. M. 2005. Linking organizational resources and work engagement to employee performance and customer loyalty: The mediation of service climate. *Journal of Applied Psychology*, 90, 1217.

Schaufeli, W. B. 2013. What is engagement? *In:* Truss, C., Delbridge, R., Alfes, K., Shantz, A., and Soane, E. (eds.) *Employee engagement in theory and practice.* New York, NY: Routledge.

Schaufeli, W. B., and Bakker, A. B. 2003. *Utrecht work engagement scale: Preliminary manual.* Utrecht: Utrecht University, 26.

Schaufeli, W. B., and Bakker, A. B. 2004. Job demands, job resources, and their relationship with burnout and engagement: A multi-sample study. *The International Journal of Industrial, Occupational Organizational Psychology Behavior*, 25, 293–315.

Schaufeli, W. B., Bakker, A. B., and Salanova, M. 2006. The measurement of work engagement with a short questionnaire: A cross-national study. *Educational and Psychological Measurement*, 66, 701–716.

Schaufeli, W. B., and De Witte, H. 2017. Outlook work engagement: Real and redundant! *Burnout Research*, 58–60.

Schaufeli, W. B., Maassen, G. H., Bakker, A. B., and Sixma, H. J. 2011. Stability and change in burnout: A 10-year follow-up study among primary care physicians. *Journal of Occupational and Organizational Psychology*, 84, 248–267.

Schaufeli, W. B., Salanova, M., González-Romá, V., and Bakker, A. B. 2002. The measurement of engagement and burnout: A two sample confirmatory factor analytic approach. *Journal of Happiness Studies*, 3, 71–92.

Schaufeli, W. B., Taris, T. W., and Van Rhenen, W. 2008. Workaholism, burnout, and work engagement: Three of a kind or three different kinds of employee well-being? *Applied Psychology*, 57, 173–203.

Scott, R. 2017. Employee engagement is declining worldwide. *Forbes.*

Scrima, F., Lorito, L., Parry, E., and Falgares, G. 2013. The mediating role of work engagement on the relationship between job involvement and affective commitment. *The International Journal of Human Resource Management*, 1–15.

Sheridan, K. 2017. *Employee engagement: The disengaged employee.* Association for Talent Development.

Shimazu, A., Schaufeli, W. B., Kubota, K., and Kawakami, N. 2012. Do workaholism and work engagement predict employee well-being and performance in opposite directions? *Industrial Health*, 50, 316–321.

Shuck, A. L., Shuck, B., and Reio, T. G. 2013a. Emotional labor and performance in the field of Child Life: Initial model exploration and implications for practice. *Children's Health Care*, 42, 168–190.

Shuck, B. 2011. Four emerging perspectives of employee engagement: An integrative literature review. *Human Resource Development Review*, 10, 304–328.

Shuck, B. 2018. Being invited in and the principle of the cumulative effect. *New Horizons in Adult Education and Human Resource Development*, 30, 1–2.

Shuck, B., Adelson, J. L., and Reio, T. G. 2017a. The employee engagement scale: Initial evidence for construct validity and implications for theory and practice. *Human Resource Management*, 56, 953–977.

Shuck, B., Alagaraja, M., Rose, K., Owen, J., Osam, K., and Bergman, M. 2017b. The health-related upside of employee engagement: Exploratory evidence and implications for theory and practice. *Performance Improvement Quarterly*, 30, 165–178.

Shuck, B., Collins, J. C., Rocco, T. S., and Diaz, R. 2016a. Deconstructing the privilege and power of employee engagement issues of inequality for management and human resource development. *Human Resource Development Review*, 15, 208–229.

Shuck, B., Ghosh, R., Zigarmi, D., and Nimon, K. 2013b. The jingle jangle of employee engagement: Further exploration of the emerging construct and implications for workplace learning and performance. *Human Resource Development Review*, 12, 11–35.

Shuck, B., Nimon, K., and Zigarmi, D. 2016b. Untangling the predictive nomological validity of employee engagement decomposing variance in employee engagement using job attitude measures. *Group & Organization Management*, 42(1). doi:1059601116642364.

Shuck, B., Osam, K., Zigarmi, D., and Nimon, K. 2017c. Definitional and conceptual muddling: Identifying the positionality of employee engagement and defining the construct. *Human Resource Development Review*, 16, 263–293.

Shuck, B., and Reio, T. G. 2014. Employee engagement and well-being: A moderation model and implications for practice. *Journal of Leadership & Organizational Studies*, 21, 43–58.

Shuck, B., Reio, T. G., and Rocco, T. S. 2011a. Employee engagement: An antecedent and outcome approach to model development. *Human Resource Development International*, 14, 427–445.

Shuck, B., Rocco, T. S., and Albornoz, C. A. 2011b. Exploring employee engagement from the employee perspective: Implications for HRD. *Journal of European Industrial Training*, 35, 300–325.

Shuck, B., and Rose, K. 2013. Reframing employee engagement within the context of meaning and purpose: Implications for HRD. *Advances in Developing Human Resources*, 15, 341–355.

Shuck, B., Twyford, D., Reio, T. G., and Shuck, A. 2014. Human resource development practices and employee engagement: Examining the connection with employee turnover intentions. *Human Resource Development Quarterly*, 25, 239–270.

Shuck, B., and Wollard, K. 2010. Employee engagement and HRD: A seminal review of the foundations. *Human Resource Development Review*, 9, 89–110.

Shuck, B., Zigarmi, D., and Owen, J. 2015. Psychological needs, engagement, and work intentions: A Bayesian multi-measurement mediation approach and implications for HRD. *European Journal of Training and Development*, 39, 2–21.

Slater, P. E. 1966. *Microcosm: Structural, psychological, and religious evolution in groups*. Hoboken, NJ: Wiley.

Smith, K. K., and Berg, D. N. 1987. *Paradoxes of group life: Understanding conflict, paralysis, and movement in group dynamics*. San Francisco, CA: Jossey-Bass.

Soane, E., Shantz, A., Alfes, K., Truss, C., Rees, C., and Gatenby, M. 2013. The association of meaningfulness, well-being, and engagement with absenteeism: A moderated mediation model. *Human Resource Management*, 52, 441–456.

Soane, E., Truss, C., Alfes, K., Shantz, A., Rees, C., and Gatenby, M. 2012. Development and application of a new measure of employee engagement: The ISA Engagement Scale. *Human Resource Development International*, 15, 529–547.

Sonnentag, S. 2012. Psychological detachment from work during leisure time: The benefits of mentally disengaging from work. *Current Directions in Psychological Science*, 21, 114–118.

Sonnentag, S., Dormann, C., and Demerouti, E. 2010. Not all days are created equal: The concept of state work engagement. *In:* Bakker, A. B., and Leiter, M. P. (eds.) *Work engagement: Recent developments in theory and research*. New York, NY: Psychology Press.

Sonnentag, S., Mojza, E. J., Binnewies, C., and Scholl, A. 2008. Being engaged at work and detached at home: A week-level study on work engagement, psychological detachment, and affect. *Work Stress and Health*, 22, 257–276.

Sonnentag, S., Mojza, E. J., Demerouti, E., and Bakker, A. B. 2012. Reciprocal relations between recovery and work engagement: The moderating role of job stressors. *Journal of Applied Psychology*, 97, 842.

Sprang, G., Clark, J. J., and Whitt-Woosley, A. 2007. Compassion fatigue, compassion satisfaction, and burnout: Factors impacting a professional's quality of life. *Journal of Loss and Trauma*, 12, 259–280.

Svendsen, M., and Joensson, T. S. 2016. Transformational leadership and change related voice behavior. *Leadership & Organization Development Journal*, 37, 357–368.

Svendsen, M., Jønsson, T. S., and Unterrainer, C. 2016. Participative supervisory behavior and the importance of feeling safe and competent to voice. *Journal of Personnel Psychology*.

Tangirala, S., and Ramanujam, R. 2012. Ask and you shall hear (but not always): Examining the relationship between manager consultation and employee voice. *Personnel Psychology*, 65, 251–282.

Thoits, P. A. 1991. On merging identity theory and stress research. *Social Psychology Quarterly*, 54(2), 101–112.

Thoresen, C. J., Kaplan, S. A., Barsky, A. P., Warren, C. R., and De Chermont, K. 2003. The affective underpinnings of job perceptions and attitudes: A meta-analytic review and integration. *17th Annual Conference of the Society for Industrial and Organizational Psychology*. Toronto, ON, Canada: American Psychological Association, 914–945.

Tims, M., Bakker, A. B., and Xanthopoulou, D. 2011. Do transformational leaders enhance their followers' daily work engagement? *The Leadership Quarterly*, 22, 121–131.

Truss, C., Alfes, K., Delbridge, R., Shantz, A., and Soane, E. 2013a. *Employee engagement in theory and practice*. Abingdon, UK: Routledge.

Truss, C., Shantz, A., Soane, E., Alfes, K., and Delbridge, R. 2013b. Employee engagement, organisational performance and individual well-being: Exploring the evidence, developing the theory. *The International Journal of Human Resource Management*, 24, 2657–2669.

Tzeng, O. C. 1975. Differentiation of affective and denotative meaning systems and their influence in personality ratings. *Journal of Personality and Social Psychology*, 32, 978–988.

Ugwu, F. O., and Onyishi, I. E. 2018. Linking perceived organizational frustration to work engagement: The moderating roles of sense of calling and psychological meaningfulness. *Journal of Career Assessment*, 26, 220–239.

Valentin, C. 2014. Employee engagement interventions: HRD, groups and teams. *In:* Walton, J., and Valentin, C. (eds.) *Human resource development: Practices and orthodoxies*. New York, NY: Palgrave Macmillan.

Vance, R. J. 2006. *Employee engagement and commitment*. Alexandria, VA: SHRM Foundation.

Vera, M., Salanova, M., and Martín, B. 2010. University faculty and work-related well-being: The importance of the triple work profile. Electronic Journal of Research in Educational Psychology, 8, 581–602.

Vroom, V. H. 1962. Egoinvolvement, job satisfaction, and job performance. *Personnel Psychology*, 15, 159–177.

Wagner, R. 2015. *Widgets: The 12 new rules for managing your employees as if they're real people*. New York, NY: McGraw Hill Professional.

Wagner, R., and Harter, J. K. 2006. *12: The elements of great managing*. New York, NY: Gallup Press.

Wefald, A. J., Reichard, R. J., and Serrano, S. A. 2011. Fitting engagement into a nomological network the relationship of engagement to leadership and personality. *Journal of Leadership & Organizational Studies*, 18, 522–537.

Wildermuth, C., and Mello, C. 2010. The personal side of engagement: The influence of personality factors. *Handbook of Employee Engagement: Perspectives, Issues, Research and Practice, Edward Elgar Publishers, Cheltenham*, 197–217.

Wildermuth, M. 2008. 10 Ms of Employee Engagement. *T and D*, 62, 50.

Wollard, K. K. 2011. Quiet desperation: Another perspective on employee engagement. *Advances in Developing Human Resources*, 13, 526–537.

Wollard, K. K., and Shuck, B. 2011. Antecedents to employee engagement: A structured review of the literature. *Advances in Developing Human Resources*, 13, 429–446.

Xanthopoulou, D., Bakker, A. B., Demerouti, E., and Schaufeli, W. B. 2009. Work engagement and financial returns: A diary study on the role of job and personal resources. *Journal of Occupational and Organizational Psychology*, 82, 183–200.

Xanthopoulou, D., Bakker, A. B., and Ilies, R. 2012. Everyday working life: Explaining within-person fluctuations in employee well-being. *Human relations*, 65, 1051–1069.

Yalabik, Z. Y., Popaitoon, P., Chowne, J. A., and Rayton, B. A. 2013. Work engagement as a mediator between employee attitudes and outcomes. *The International Journal of Human Resource Management*, 24, 2799–2823.

Yalabik, Z. Y., Rayton, B. A., and Rapti, A. 2017. Facets of job satisfaction and work engagement. *Evidence-based HRM: A Global Forum for Empirical Scholarship*, 5(3), 248–265. Emerald Publishing Limited.

Ybema, S., Keenoy, T., Oswick, C., Beverungen, A., Ellis, N., and Sabelis, I. 2009. Articulating identities. *Human Relations*, 62, 299–322.

Yildirim, I. 2008. Relationships between burnout, sources of social support and sociodemographic variables. *Social Behavior and Personality: An International Journal*, 36, 603–616.

Young, H. R., Glerum, D. R., Wang, W., and Joseph, D. 2018. Who are the most engaged at work? A meta-analysis of personality and employee engagement. *Journal of Organizational Behavior*, 39, 1330–1346.

Zajonc, R. B. 1980. Feeling and thinking: Preferences need no inferences. *American Psychologist*, 35, 151–175.

Zhu, W., He, H., Treviño, L. K., Chao, M. M., and Wang, W. 2015. Ethical leadership and follower voice and performance: The role of follower identifications and entity morality beliefs. *The Leadership Quarterly*, 26, 702–718.

Zigarmi, D., and Nimon, K. 2011. A cognitive approach to work intention: The stuff that employee work passion is made of? *Advances in Developing Human Resources*, 13, 447–461.

Zigarmi, D., Nimon, K., Houson, D., Witt, D., and Diehl, J. 2011. A preliminary field test of an employee work passion model. *Human Resource Development Quarterly*, 22, 195–221.

Index

Page numbers in *italic* indicate a figure on the corresponding page. Page numbers in **bold** indicate a table on the corresponding page.

Printed in the United States
by Baker & Taylor Publisher Services